SETTING UP AND RUNNING A THERAPY BUSINESS

SETTING UP AND RUNNING A THERAPY BUSINESS
Frequently Asked Questions

James Rye

Routledge
Taylor & Francis Group

LONDON AND NEW YORK

First published 2017 by
Karnac Books Ltd.

Published 2018 by Routledge
2 Park Square, Milton Park, Abingdon, Oxon OX14 4RN
711 Third Avenue, New York, NY 10017, USA

*Routledge is an imprint of the Taylor & Francis Group,
an informa business*

British Library Cataloguing in Publication Data

A C.I.P. for this book is available from the British Library

ISBN-13: 9781782204640 (pbk)

Typeset by V Publishing Solutions Pvt Ltd., Chennai, India

CONTENTS

ACKNOWLEDGEMENTS   xiii

ABOUT THE AUTHOR   xvii

Starting up

1   Why should I consider private practice?   3
Benefits for counsellors   4
Benefits for clients   5
A word of caution   7

2   What qualifications, experience, and qualities
do I need to start a private practice?   9
Professional qualifications and experience   9
Personal qualities   11

3   What things must I do if I go self-employed?   15
Register with HMRC   15
Keep financial records   16

4   What should I consider if planning to work
from home?   17
Interruptions   17

Disruption to others   18
Safety   19
Waiting rooms and bathrooms   20
Legal and financial considerations   20
Disability discrimination act   21
Non-verbal messages   22
Miscellany   23

5 What should I consider if planning to hire
a room?   25
Costs?   25
Other questions relating to cost   26
Location?   27
Accessibility?   27
Dual usage?   27

6 What insurance do I need as a private
practitioner?   31
Professional liability insurance   31
Working from home   32
Home contents insurance (business usage)   32
Home building insurance (business usage)   33
Working from a hired room   33
Motor vehicle insurance (business usage)   34
Legitimate business expenditure   34

Money issues

7 How much should I charge?   37

8 How much can I expect to earn?   41

9 How can I accept payment?   45
Cash   45
Cheque   46
Bank transfer   46
Mobile phone payment (PayM)   47
Credit/debit card   47

10 Should I give the first session for free? 51
Reasons for doing so 51
Reasons for not doing so 52
You decide 53

11 Should I charge for sessions when a client
doesn't turn up or cancels with short notice? 55
Reasons for non-attendance or insufficient
cancellation 56
To charge or not to charge 57
Advance payment 59
Working for EAPs and other companies 60

12 What are business expenses, and why do
I need to bother about them? 63
What are business expenses? 64
Communication and running an office
expenses 64
Professional fees and personal development
expenses 66
An example business 66
Two continuing professional development (CPD)
events 68
The network meeting 68
The day conference 69
Paying less tax 70

Marketing

13 What are your tips for marketing my
business? (1) 75
Why? 75
What? 76

14 What are your tips for marketing my
business? (2) 81
Where? 81

Be particularly cautious about ...   82
Other options   84

15   What else can I do to help my business grow? 89
Specialisation   90
Increased income streams   92
Increased access   93
Putting it together   94

Other practical issues

16   What can I do to increase my personal
safety when working alone?   97
Initial screening   98
Avoiding misunderstanding   99
Further possible practical steps   100

17   Do I need to give clients a written contract? 103
Private practitioners are isolated   103
Working ethically   104

18   If I issue a written contract, what might
it include?   107
An example contract   108
Counselling Agreement   108
Agreement between XXX and XXX   108
Appointments   108
The sessions   109
Fees   111
Additional work   112
Health   112
Cancellation   112
Confidentiality   113
Record-keeping   114
Other responsibilities as a client   116
Review   116
Jurisdiction   116

19 How could I introduce a written contract?   119

20 How can I store my notes?   123
Physical notes   123
Electronic notes   124
Computer storage   124
Cloud storage   125

21 Do I need to register with the Information
        Commissioner's Office?   129
The self-assessment   131
The misconceptions   132
Hand-written material   132
The European Economic Area   133

22 What about working for agencies?   135
Employee assistance providers   135
Rehabilitation agencies and solicitors   137
Other companies   137
Number of sessions (short-term work)   138
The messy but important details   139
How can I get such work?   140

23 Can I work with clients in their own homes?   143
Insurance   144
Costs   145
Safety   147
Conditions   148
Access   149
Alternatives   150

24 Will I have to work evenings and weekends?   151

25 What should I do if I bump into my clients
        in my locality?   155
A professional relationship   156
Empower the client   157
The awkward two   157

26 How can I increase the chances of an enquiry
      becoming a client?   159
Helping secure a first appointment   159
Review the telephone contact options   160
Possible booking solutions   162
Speed and redundancy   164
Listening to need   165

Miscellany

27 How can I get a website?   169
Website designers   169
Online website builders   171
Search engine optimisation   172

28 What are outcome measures and should
      I use them?   175
What measures could I use?   180
PHQ-9   180
GAD-7   181
CORE-10   181
Satisfaction with life scale   181
WEMWBS   181
QIDS-SR16   182
NovoPsych   182

29 What is a professional will and do
      I need one?   185

30 How can I increase access to my services?   189
Sally's story   192
Maryanne and Tom's story   193
Increasing access   194

31 What is the difference between a sole
      trader and a limited company?   197
Liability   198

Flexibility   198
Registration and paperwork   199
Expense   200
Seek advice   200

ACKNOWLEDGEMENTS

Many people have unwittingly contributed to this book.

I first tentatively started out in private practice in 1997 and am grateful to the thousands of clients whom I have seen since then who have made me think through problems and attempt to come up with solutions. Their presence and absence pushed me to try to find answers to diverse and mundane questions such as: Why aren't more clients coming to my door and what can I do about it? Why can't I accept credit card payments? What can and can't I claim against tax? And in later years, as my business and experience grew, those questions have been sharpened by supervising several counsellors who wanted clear answers to practical questions.

From 2010 to 2015, I had the privilege of serving on the Executive Committee of BACP Private Practice Division (latterly as its chair). During those years, I spent many hours in meetings in London and at BACP headquarters in Lutterworth trying to identify the needs of private practitioners, and trying to help BACP continue to be an organisation that could meet some of those needs. I am truly grateful to my sometime fellow committee members and practitioners: Rabina Akhtar, John Crew, John Daniel, Julia Greer, Wendy Halsall, Martin Hogg, Mervyn Wynn Jones, Meg Logan, Susan Utting-Simon, Patti Wallace, Guy Westoby. I greatly valued their contribution to the hours of professional discussion, their challenges and support, and their ability to laugh. Some of my views on private practice were enlightened by those discussions.

During my years on the committee, two other important things happened. First, part of my responsibility involved representing the Private Practice Division at numerous BACP training events in various parts of the country. At every event I attended, I met many people—some experienced counsellors, some just starting out—but nearly all of them asking questions: Can I do this? How do I do that? Do I have to do that? It was a powerful reminder that we train people to do professional therapy, but we do not train therapy professionals to run businesses. It left me with a desire to do something to try to fill that gap.

The second important thing was that John Daniel— the editor of the BACP journal *The Independent Practitioner*, which then became *Private Practice*—was also on the Executive Committee. He gave me opportunity and encouragement to write down some of my thoughts about private practice. Some of the material for three of the answers in this book—How much can I expect to earn? How can I increase the chances of an enquiry becoming a client? How can I increase access to my services?—originally appeared as articles in the above journals. They are reprinted here with the kind permission of the BACP, who also gave permission to quote from their revised ethical framework.

I am also greatly indebted to my wife, Nina, who as a practising therapist herself brings me down to earth, shares her immense wisdom, and has patiently supported me over the past twenty years, despite the disruption caused by running a business from home.

I wish to clearly state that the views presented in this book are my own and do not represent the views of any particular organisation. The information is offered in good faith, but you are encouraged to seek the advice of other professionals (such as an accountant and business advisor) when making important decisions that affect your own business.

ABOUT THE AUTHOR

James Rye has been working as a counsellor in private practice since 1997. He formed Connections Counselling Ltd in 2002 and became a partner in Peterborough Counsellor Training in 2012. He now works as a counsellor/psychotherapist, clinical supervisor, and trainer. Right from the start of his counselling career, the author has worked with clients via telephone and online, as well as face to face, and now regularly interacts therapeutically with a wide client base, drawn from his local community, from the whole of the UK, and from ex-pats abroad.

In 2010, the author was invited on to the Executive Committee of the BACP Private Practice Division, and he served as chair of that committee from 2013 to 2015. His committee role involved visiting many parts of the UK to attend training events, promoting the Private Practice Division, and answering questions from people about setting up and running a business as a counsellor.

Before finally leaving the world of education in 2001, the author had worked for thirty years as a teacher and manager in secondary schools, and in further and higher education.

He lives in King's Lynn, is married, and has two grown-up children.

Starting up

CHAPTER ONE

Why should I consider private practice?

L et's be honest, a lot of therapists end up in private practice almost by default rather than by enthusiastic choice. Many enter years of training with a genuine but vague notion of "wanting to help people". And then, years later, they realise that there are very few paid counselling jobs available, and at this point, a significant number of trained counsellors effectively "disappear" and never directly use their expensively acquired skills as a means of generating income.

For those who are determined to try to earn money from their training, they now face what is for many the unwanted task of setting up and running a business. Although there are those who, right from the beginning, relish the prospect of working for themselves, I strongly suspect that they are in the minority. For most of us in private practice, the genuine relishing comes after experience and growth in confidence. However, regardless of whether we are initially reluctant or very willing business owners, there are a number of compelling reasons for considering starting a private practice.

Benefits for counsellors

The benefits to counsellors are those that accrue to all people who are self-employed. They are the increased freedom of choice and power to control when and where you work, and, to some extent, how much you get paid. If you don't want to drive to an office, you could choose to work from home. If you don't want to work on a Wednesday afternoon, you can choose not to do so. If you want to work part time, you can set your own working hours. If you want a pay rise, you can try to raise your prices.

Although, as we shall see, there is a cost to that freedom of choice and power, for many people there are also very strong psychological benefits. Most counsellors enter the profession after a number of years in paid employment, and they enjoy the freedom of being their own boss, especially if they have suffered from working for whimsical, capricious, rude, or bullying superiors.

Before becoming a self-employed counsellor, I spent many years in educational management. For some of that time, I performed tasks that I enjoyed, and on other occasions, I performed tasks that I didn't enjoy but which I knew were necessary. However, on other occasions, I performed tasks that were legal but with which I profoundly disagreed. I knew that I had to do them if I wished to keep my job and continue to pay the mortgage. And when in middle management, I occasionally felt that my creativity and problem-solving abilities were thwarted. I rightly had to yield to my seniors, who sometimes didn't share my views, my solutions, my timescales, my willingness to take risks, or my confidence in my ability to deliver what was required, or to adapt to and successfully manage any failure.

Now I genuinely enjoy running my own business. I am free from the office politics. Looking back over nearly twenty years, I have a real sense of satisfaction that I have been able to create something worthwhile that regularly generates important income for me. I enjoy the freedom I have to plan and make changes that I want to make. It pleases me to be able to try out things and take appropriate and measured risks to see if things work out in a business sense. Self-employment has enabled me to express parts of my personality that were, of necessity, being curtailed while I was being employed by someone else.

Benefits for clients

Although most readers of this book will be thinking about the possible advantages of working in private practice from a personal point of view, there are many potential benefits for clients in having a large number of competent private practitioners available. In a recent paper, Patti Wallace, the then BACP Lead Advisor for Private Practice, cogently set out the many potential benefits of having a large number of private practitioners available to clients ("The contribution of private practice counselling", BACP 2015). Wallace lists nine potential benefits for the client of working with a private practitioner as opposed to working with a counsellor employed by an organisation (such as the NHS). I have added a tenth.

- Choice of person. If they wish to, clients have the freedom to choose a therapist on the basis of gender, age, sexual orientation, race, spoken language, level of training and/or experience, and experience of, or interest in, particular issues.

- Choice of location. Clients may not wish to travel far for therapy. Alternatively, they may wish to have a counsellor outside of their local geographical area.
- Choice of timing. Clients may not wish to be constrained by the usual norms of a working week and may have difficulty in keeping daytime appointments. They are free to seek out private practitioners who offer evening and weekend appointments if they wish to do so.
- Choice of counselling model. While it may be true that most clients are unaware of the variety of counselling models available, some are aware and have a particular choice. So, for example, because of recommendations from a GP, it is not uncommon for clients to specifically seek out a therapist who offers EMDR or CBT.
- Reduced waiting time. Most clients would have to wait weeks, if not months, for an NHS counselling appointment (even if one were available). By selecting a private practitioner, clients who can afford to pay rarely have to wait more than a week.
- Help without a diagnosis. Clients who work in certain sectors (in the NHS, or in the military, for example) often fear having anything to do with mental health, and especially a mental health diagnosis on their medical record, for fear that such information would hinder their careers. Records kept by private practitioners are not part of any formal NHS medical record.
- Greater confidentiality. However secure records are, people who go for a counselling appointment in an organisation are sometimes unsure about how many people will have access to their records. When going to a good private practitioner, clients know there is usually less risk of accidental or systematic leakage.

- Less disclosure of risk. Counsellors working for, or within, organisations must follow the rules of that organisation about the disclosure of risk. Counsellors working for the NHS, for example, have to disclose concerns about serious risk to other relevant professionals, whether or not the client agrees to that. There is no such compulsion for private practitioners to do so. Some would want to do so anyway and would communicate their policy on disclosure in their initial contract. However, others are willing to keep that risk confidential for as long as the client asks them to do so.
- Empowered customers. Clients who pay for counselling are customers as well as clients. Their decision to choose a therapist, to choose a number of sessions, and to choose to pay gives them a lot more power in the relationship than clients being told who to see and for how long. The clients have much more autonomy.
- Choice of counselling modality. Although the counselling profession as a whole has been slow to embrace the use of modern technology, more and more therapists are now using technology to offer sessions in a variety of ways. Face-to-face communication is no longer the only option. Clients can elect to have telephone sessions, voice chat over the internet, video sessions, and therapy via instant messaging. At the time of writing, it is predominantly private practitioners who are offering these choices.

A word of caution

Of course, not everything in the private practice garden is automatically rosy. Research published by the Social Market Foundation recently found that the proportion of low-paid self-employed, based on both hourly and monthly earnings, has increased significantly since the recession. Around fifty-five per cent of the self-employed have monthly incomes that are less than two-thirds of median employee earnings (https://flipchartfairytales.wordpress.com/2016/03/22/self-employed-slide-further-into-poverty/).

Starting out as a therapist, especially if you have no other sources of immediate income, can be financially challenging. Also, self-employed practitioners don't have the benefits of working closely with other colleagues and of feeling part of a therapeutic team. They often feel isolated. They do not have the security of a regular income or a substantial work pension, and thus carry the responsibility for having to generate income (week-in, week-out), pay taxes, and face any consequences of failing to do so. They often work unsocial hours. Organisations tend to have many support structures in place, and private practitioners often face greater risk without them.

One of the purposes of this book is to help readers avoid some of the pitfalls and enjoy creating something of significant benefit to others and to themselves.

CHAPTER TWO

What qualifications, experience, and qualities do I need to start a private practice?

Professional qualifications and experience

As most of you will be aware, at the time of writing "counselling" and "psychotherapy" are not yet protected titles, and anyone can claim to be a counsellor or psychotherapist (and sadly, some very unqualified people do). Similarly, there are no "rules" governing who can and who can't set up in private practice.

However, having said that, there are two things that potential practitioners would do well to consider when trying to reach a decision on the matter.

The first is the ethical code of their professional body. Whichever professional association you belong to, it will almost certainly contain a requirement that therapists work in the best interests of the client. The question for would-be private practitioners is: "Do I feel reasonably confident that my level of training and experience is sufficient for me to genuinely work in the best interests of the client?"

Many counsellors starting out may not be able to give a simple, clear answer to that question. A lot would depend on the type and number of clients they saw. Perhaps they would feel that they could do a good job if they saw a few, relatively "uncomplicated" clients (whatever that means) each week, but they would acknowledge that if they started to see a large number of clients with very "complex" needs, they would struggle to feel that they were the right people to work with them.

In reality, when starting out, new private practitioners are very unlikely to immediately start seeing large numbers of clients each week. And if they had a clear process for screening clients, and for referring on when necessary, that may be a way for some to start, very tentatively, dipping a toe in the private practice water with a degree of professional integrity.

The second valuable source of help in reaching a decision about whether or not you are sufficiently qualified and experienced is your supervisor. A good supervisor who knows your existing work will be able to be congruent with their judgement about whether she or he feels you are sufficiently professionally competent to take the risk of starting to work without the support of an organisation around you. Some private practitioners ensure that they have extra supervision when starting out, as a way of trying to safeguard their clients.

Put simply, you should try to have the best available training as a counsellor and the longest possible period of practice after training before working independently. Some individuals have regarded BACP accreditation (or the equivalent from other counselling organisations) as an appropriate benchmark to achieve before feeling happy about working in private practice. Similarly, some employee assistance providers, insurance companies, and rehabilitation agencies (a significant source of income for private practitioners) would not award counselling contracts to therapists who did not have accreditation.

Personal qualities

Starting and running a business is not for everybody, and would-be private practitioners would do well to be realistic about their own personal strengths and weaknesses before embarking on such a venture. Apart from the professional difficulties of working with clients in an isolated context, there are the personal qualities that are needed to overcome other difficulties.

First, there is the business context. At the time of writing, the market appears to be flooded with counsellors. In an ideal world, the training providers would look at the needs of the nation and come up with a figure of how many new counsellors were needed to meet that need, and then allocate the requisite number of training places each year. In practice, training providers are concerned with maintaining their own financial stability and with selling training places, regardless of need. When you add to that the fact that there are many institutions and organisations (not necessarily all of the highest quality) offering varying lengths of training, it is relatively easy to get a piece of paper saying you have "done a counselling course" and to call yourself a "counsellor". There are lots of private practitioners fishing in the same pond for clients, and the number of practitioners is growing. It takes a certain amount of skill and determination to stand out from the crowd and to successfully and regularly attract a significant number of paying clients.

Second, there are the qualities needed to deal with the everyday challenges of running the business itself.

- Am I an organised person? What evidence is there that I am prepared to do (and perhaps, even enjoy) administration? Could I cope with regular filing of a large amount of paperwork, or am I sufficiently IT competent to keep secure electronic records? If my practice grows, and I start to regularly see four or five clients during a day, not only are there the pro-fessional client notes and contracts to deal with, but there is a plethora of other administration: dealing with the enquiries that have come in by email during the day; responding to voicemail messages; record-ing the accounts; banking money; completing diary entries; completing the necessary client paperwork for each Employee Assistance Provider (EAP) that you work for. I spend between one and two hours each day doing administration, in addition to any cli-ent contact.
- Would people who know me well consider that I am moderately numerically and financially literate? If I am not happy with figures, am I prepared to pay someone else to do that, or am I prepared to learn how to use a simple accounting package to keep track of my income and expenses? Would I be able to tell whether the business was making a profit or a loss, and what the amount of any profit or loss would be?
- Do I want to shoulder the responsibility for the suc-cess or failure of what happens? Am I strong enough to take the risk?
- Because it may take time to build up financial suc-cess, do I have the patience to take a longer-term view? Do I have sufficient alternative financial resources to enable me to do that?
- Would my former work colleagues judge that I am sufficiently flexible and creative to work at trying

out alternative strategies if things don't immediately work out first time? Would they think that I give up too easily?

- Am I able to work independently and vary my routine according to needs?
- Would any partner that I might have consider that I am able to be proactive, or would they consider that I have to wait until I am forced to do something that I would rather avoid?

* * *

Although it is important to be realistic about the difficulties, and although it is true that many businesses fold within the first two years, it is also true that a large number of counsellors are making all or part of their living by practising privately. I suspect that many may not be looking to generate a large salary, have other sources of income, and would be content with "part-time" work. Nevertheless, there are counsellors out there who are totally dependent on their business for a living. It is possible to earn a living as a private practitioner.

CHAPTER THREE

What things must I do if I go self-employed?

Register with HMRC

Within three months of starting trading, you must register with HMRC. You will be responsible for paying any tax liabilities and you will be liable for National Insurance contributions (Class 2 and Class 4). You are advised to seek professional advice from an accountant who can take note of your particular liabilities that are likely to be affected by other factors (for example, work history, business structure, turnover, other income).

Upon registration, you'll need to provide the following information:

address
National Insurance number
date of birth
telephone number
email address
the nature of your business
start date of self-employment

business address

business telephone number

your Unique Tax Reference (UTR)—only if you were within self-assessment previously

the business's UTR—if you're joining an existing partnership

if relevant, the full name and date of birth of any business partners.

It is unlikely that your turnover will be sufficiently large for you to need to register for VAT (£83,000 in 2016).

See: http://www.hmrc.gov.uk/startingup/index.htm

Keep financial records

You must keep up-to-date and accurate records of all your transactions—who pays you what, and who you pay, and for what. Some people prefer to do this by keeping a physical book, others use a spreadsheet, others teach themselves how to use a simple accounts program that does all the calculations at the press of a button and usually produces simple reports that inform you of how much profit or loss you are making. Clear, accurate information will keep the tax authorities happy and make it easier to run your business.

CHAPTER FOUR

What should I consider if planning to work from home?

For some counsellors, working from home is the last thing they would want to do. The idea of clients knowing where they live seems repugnant, unprofessional, and possibly even threatening. However, for others, it may initially seem an attractive, "easy" option. It may seem to require less effort (you don't have to go in search of suitable premises), and it may also seem less risky financially (you don't have to agree to any rental contract for a minimum period). In some ways, it is more convenient: there is no travelling involved, and if a client fails to turn up (which can happen a significant number of times), you can simply carry on with your normal daily life.

Despite any initial attractions that working from home may have, there are several important things to consider before making that choice.

Interruptions

How would you prevent (or aim to prevent) the normal interruptions to domestic life that take place in a home from disturbing your therapy sessions? What about:

17

- The phone that frequently rings unexpectedly?
- The postie that can't fit the parcel through the letterbox and wants your attention?
- The friend who seems to have forgotten that you do serious work from home and drops by on the off-chance that you might want to go out for a coffee?
- The window cleaner who suddenly appears unannounced outside your therapy room and starts to clean the windows during one of your sessions and then knocks on the outside door expecting to be paid?
- The gardener who unexpectedly appears with a petrol lawnmower and proceeds to cut the grass?
- The members from a political party or from a religious group who knock on your door wanting to engage you in a serious conversation?
- The double-glazing sales person?

It is possible to handle all of the above with planning. You can unplug phones or forward calls to voicemail or an answerphone, or to an answering service. You can ignore demands to go to the front door and even put up "Do not disturb" signs. You can plan times with (or cancel the use of) any service providers such as window cleaners and gardeners. However, you do need to think through such eventualities.

Disruption to others

In some districts, there may be considerable inconvenience if you cannot offer clients off-road parking. Some neighbours are not likely to take too kindly to a continual (or even an occasional) stream of unfamiliar vehicles filling up the limited parking spaces in front of their houses for long periods of time.

Working from home can mean considerable disruption to family life. If you do not live alone, you need to think through what will happen to other family members and how they will respond 1) if the phone rings, and 2) when clients come to the house. You will need systems for dealing professionally with phone calls (see "How can I increase the chances of enquiries becoming clients?"), and you will need to ensure that other family members are not around immediately before, during, or after sessions. Partners may tolerate being occasionally banned to the kitchen or bedroom, but might object to that in the long term, and teenage children will certainly protest loudly. Depending on your family situation and the size of your house, the solution may be to work only during the hours when the house can be guaranteed to be empty of other occupants (bearing in mind that such a decision, however necessary, will inevitably affect your availability and therefore your income).

You also need to think about and "test" whether or not the walls of your therapy room are sound-proof. You don't want to have sessions interrupted by conversations, music, or TV programmes leaking in from elsewhere in the house. And clients need to be protected from other household members being able to hear what is being discussed in confidence in your work room.

Safety

If choosing to work from home, you are making a conscious decision to invite complete strangers, some of whom may have serious mental health issues, into your house. In a busy practice, that can involve you in working with hundreds, even thousands, of people over the years. You will need to take sensible precautions to minimise risk. See "What can I do to increase my personal safety when working alone?".

Waiting rooms and bathrooms

Most counsellors working from home would not be able to provide a waiting room if clients were to arrive early (which some of them frequently do, especially when nervous about a first appointment). And even if you have a suitable room, it may not be advisable to leave an unattended stranger there, or have to disrupt your therapy session early in order to go to the door to let the next client in. The lack of a waiting room and your unavailability to answer the door before time needs to be made clear to clients before they attend the first session.

Some clients will ask to use your bathroom, so you also need to think about the state of the rooms they would have to pass through, and the condition of the bathroom itself, in order to avoid embarrassment.

Legal and financial considerations

If you decide to work from home, you will probably need to inform your local council planning department, though you are unlikely to require special planning permission. The planning department is usually happy to allow you to work from home by accepting auxiliary usage for the property. However, it is likely to stipulate that the change must not result in "heavy usage" (significantly large numbers of customers coming and going), and no signage would be allowed.

If you have a mortgage, it would be wise to check with the mortgage company and/or with a solicitor whether running a business from the property breaks one of the stipulations in the mortgage document about the property usage. Similarly, if you are renting a property, you should check your rental agreement and have an honest discussion with your landlord.

Technically, you may be liable to pay business rates on the part of the property used for the business, though in practice this is rare and depends on a review of the rateable value of the property. Because usually only one room is involved, and the room is not always exclusively used for therapy, if business rates are charged, the amount of money required can be relatively modest. (See: https://www.gov.uk/introduction-to-business-rates/working-at-home).

In addition to your professional insurance, your building and home contents insurance policies will need modifying to take on board the fact that you are working from home. (For a fuller discussion of the insurance issues, see "What insurance do I need as a private practitioner?".)

Disability discrimination act

This act makes it against the law for service providers to discriminate against disabled people on the grounds of their disability. Service providers are expected to make reasonable adjustments to facilitate disabled people. However, what is considered reasonable (practical and affordable) for a large organisation is different from what a small business operating from home might be expected to do.

In an ideal world, our homes would have ramps, doors wide enough for wheelchairs, and an accessible toilet, but it would be impractical and unaffordable for most therapists to make the necessary changes to their houses. However, while such big, physical changes are beyond the scope of many counsellors, it would be reasonable to offer to provide any written material in large print, if required; and in some cases, it might be appropriate to consider offering to conduct therapy by telephone, by video chat, or in the disabled client's home.

Non-verbal messages

As counsellors we are hopefully more aware than most of the power of non-verbal messages. We need to be aware of what working from home is "saying" about our business, and to make sure that our therapy space supports, rather than detracts from, our therapeutic work.

For some people, working from home can give off messages of "small-scale" and "amateur", even "unsuccessful". Such clients are likely to seek out a counsellor with a "proper" business address. Other clients are unworried by a home address and even welcome it; for some, it can make the visit less daunting. On the other hand, there are those who might be more anxious initially about going to spend time alone in a stranger's house, especially if they feel vulnerable; an office in a therapy centre might seem a more public and safer place.

If you work from home, I think that it is important for clients to know that you do this before they arrive. It is part of the information that helps them make an informed choice. I know of one counsellor who, when replying to the initial email or phone call from clients, and on all her publicity material, clearly states "I work from an office at home …". This helps avoid any later awkwardness and misunderstanding.

Clients will inevitably start gathering information from the moment of first contact, and especially when they enter a front door. Untidiness, a lack of cleanliness, and poor organisation are hardly likely to convey a professional image of competence that will encourage clients to trust. Therapy rooms at home need to be uncluttered and devoid of potentially distracting personal material. Photographs of a happily married couple and of children or grandchildren may be painful for clients recently separated from partners or children and for those struggling with fertility issues. Old slippers, an empty dog basket, and children's toys, although silent, can speak volumes and immediately undo the message conveyed by a professional-looking website or leaflet.

Miscellany

Having larger numbers of people in your home will inevitably increase the wear and tear on your carpets and furniture. On occasions, the floors will inevitably get more dirty than usual. You need to be prepared to do regular room, access area, and bathroom cleaning, or plan for who is going to do it.

Some people arrive with strong aromas—including, but not exclusively, perfume, aftershave, body odour, smoke—and these smells may linger and occasionally permeate adjacent rooms in the house. Equally, lingering cooking smells can be a problem when seeing clients close to a meal time.

CHAPTER FIVE

What should I consider if planning to hire a room?

There are advantages and disadvantages to hiring a room to use to conduct your business. The advantages might include a clear separation between work and private life (including family members and the likelihood of domestic interruptions), the ability to have a room furnished for and used only for therapy, and perhaps informal support from other therapists who may use the same building. The disadvantages might include greater costs, and being tied to a long-term tenancy agreement.

I have listed below some questions that you might find it useful to find answers to if you are considering renting a room to use for therapy.

Costs?

Your room cost might be charged in a variety of ways. You might be asked to pay so much per hour of actual use. Obviously such an arrangement is likely to be to your advantage, especially when starting up. However, such an arrangement is rare. If you are fortunate enough to find such an agreement, find out whether or not you have to pay for the use of the room if your client fails to arrive. You would normally be expected to do so.

You might be asked to pay so much per week, or so much per month. If this is the case, you would need to make a realistic calculation about the number of clients you will see, and whether their fees will cover the rental cost (regardless of covering any other costs). If you cannot guarantee to cover the weekly or monthly rental costs, you will need additional capital to invest in the business until it grows sufficiently to cover the rent.

Other questions relating to cost

- How much notice do I need to give if I decide to back out of the rental agreement?
- Does the rent price cover utilities such as heat, light, and water?
- Does the room have a telephone, and how is that charged for?
- Am I required to sign a long-term tenancy agreement, saying, for example, that I will pay the rent for a minimum period of six months, and if so, can I afford to do that?
- Is the room furnished appropriately, or am I required to buy furniture?
- If I found that I wasn't getting enough clients but that I was tied into a long-term agreement, how amenable would the landlord be to my sub-letting the room out to other counsellors when I wasn't able to use it?
- Is the price of cleaning the room, access area, and bathroom covered in the contract? If not, who is going to do it, and how much will it cost?

- What about insurance? The therapist would, of course, have professional liability insurance, but who is responsible for any costs associated with damage to the building or building contents? The landlord would almost certainly have building insurance, but check out whether he or she has contents. (See "What insurance do I need as a private practitioner?".)

Location?

Is the room in a location that is likely to be attractive to clients? Are there good parking facilities? If I want to use it during the evenings, is it appropriately lit? Is it in an area where people would generally feel safe, and feel safe to leave their cars?

Accessibility?

Is it easily accessible by public transport? If I wanted to use the building outside of "normal" office hours (i.e., evenings and weekends), could I and my clients get easy access?

Dual usage?

What else (if anything) and who else (if anyone) uses the same room or building? Some organisations or businesses may be willing to rent out a spare room for counsellors to use. For example, I have known counsellors hire rooms in religious buildings, community centres, or above shops. The following might be the kind of questions to ask about such rooms:

- Is the main purpose of the building likely to make it difficult for some clients to enter the building? Some clients might be happy entering a religious building, whereas others would find it extremely off-putting. If the therapist became associated with the building and the client assumed that the therapist and the religion shared the same values, then the therapy could easily break down (if it ever got started).

- Is the client able to easily and confidentially access the therapy room without other building users being aware? If your therapy room were above a hairdresser's shop, it would be extremely unsuitable if your clients had to enter the shop and run the gauntlet of customers to access the room upstairs.
- How likely is it that noise from the building will permeate and disturb the therapy? How sound-proof is the therapy room?

In some dual-usage buildings, it is not uncommon for the therapy room itself to have a dual usage at different times during the day or week. If this is the case:

- How likely is it that you might face constant interruptions to the therapy? I know of one counsellor who worked with children in an office in a school. The head was very supportive of her work and the office of a senior member of staff was vacated on several occasions during the week to enable the therapy to take place. Despite staff being aware of the times, and large signs on the door, the sessions were regularly interrupted by staff "just popping in" to get something.
- How likely is it that what else goes on in the room when you are not using it makes it difficult for you? I know of one counsellor who hired a room on a Monday in a community centre. His room was used as part of the social club that met at weekends. Every Monday he had to arrive early, open the windows

in the hallway to his room and in his room to get rid of the smell of stale beer and smoke, clear away half-drunk glasses, and generally clean and "fumigate" the room before he could use it with clients.

If your room is part of a therapy centre that is used by other counsellors, hopefully you won't encounter many of the potential problems discussed above. You may even get support from growing to be part of a therapeutic community.

CHAPTER SIX

What insurance do I need as a private practitioner?

There are several risks involved in running a private practice. What if your client feels seriously aggrieved with the therapy you have provided and decides to sue you? What if your client accidentally knocks your computer off the desk? What if you have a road accident while driving to your supervisor? Fortunately, there are insurance policies available to protect you from excessive financial risk.

Professional liability insurance

Although there is no legal requirement for you to have professional liability insurance (also known as "professional indemnity insurance", or PI), there are two compelling reasons for taking out such a policy.

First, most professional counselling organisations require you to demonstrate that you have such insurance if you are to become one of their members. Most creditable supervisors would require you to have such insurance before agreeing to supervise your work. Most EAPs and agencies would require you to demonstrate that you have such insurance before offering you work as one of their affiliates.

Second, the cost of not having it might lead most counsellors into bankruptcy or severe financial hardship. The cost of mounting a legal defence if sued, and then paying any financial compensation if you lost the case, could easily run into hundreds of thousands of pounds. Fortunately, such allegations are rare, but they do occasionally happen. Even if allegations of inadequate or harmful service are proved to be unfounded, defence costs are still likely to be significant.

If you intend to work with clients who live abroad (see "How can I increase access to my services?") make sure that your insurer is aware of this. Although some will provide cover for this work, not all will, and there may be limitations (for example, excluding clients from the USA and Canada).

Working from home

Home contents insurance (business usage)

Most practitioners would have a home contents policy covering accidental damage to the contents of their property. However, not all private practitioners inform their insurer that they are using their home to run their business, and in failing to do so, invalidate their home contents policies.

As soon as you start to run your business, you need to inform your home contents insurer. From the insurer's point of view, running a business from home increases the risk to them. If you have more people coming into your house than is the average for most people, and if most of those visitors are initially strangers (and have "mental health issues"), then statistically there is a greater risk of home contents damage and possibly of theft.

Because of this greater risk, two things may happen. First, you may be asked to pay a higher premium to take account of the increased likelihood of a claim. Second, you may find that your usual insurance company is no longer willing to insure your contents and will terminate your policy. Initially, this can feel alarming. However, most of the specialist counsellor insurance agencies would be able to put you in touch with insurance companies willing to insure your contents when working from home.

Home building insurance (business usage)

The situation with home building insurance is identical to that of home contents insurance. You need to inform your building insurers immediately of your change of usage, and again they may increase the premium or terminate the policy. And again, most of the specialist counsellor insurance agencies would be able to put you in touch with insurance companies willing to insure your building when working from home.

If you fail to inform your insurers of your business and ever needed to make a claim through your building policy, the policy would be invalid, even if a client had nothing whatsoever to do with the damage to the building.

Working from a hired room

Make sure you have a clear understanding from your landlord about who is responsible for any damage in the property. Does she or he have contents insurance for the room you are using and for the access routes you and your clients will use?

Motor vehicle insurance (business usage)

If you use your vehicle in any way in relation to your business (and most counsellors do), then again, you need to inform your insurer and expect to pay a slightly higher premium for business usage. Typical business usage would be travelling to a client, to your supervisor, or to a professional development event. Unlike with building and contents insurance, most motor vehicle insurers would be happy to insure you for business usage.

Legitimate business expenditure

The good news is that the full cost of professional liability insurance, and the higher cost difference of contents, building, and vehicle insurance, can be claimed as a business expenditure to be set against your tax liability. (See "What are business expenses and why do I need to bother about them?".)

Money issues

CHAPTER SEVEN

How much should I charge?

The issue of how much to charge is a tricky one. There are at least six factors that are relevant to the decision-making process.

First, you need to consider what your service is worth. Think about what you are offering people. Increasingly, you are likely to have graduate and even post-graduate qualifications. You are offering people a safe place for their emotions and deepest secrets. In the longer term, you are hoping to help them bring significant changes in their lives—for example, greater acceptance of self and others, better relationships, less anxiety, more freedom from dysfunctional patterns, improved functioning at home and at work. All these changes are likely to have a life-long impact. Most people would be prepared to pay several hundreds, if not thousands, of pounds in total for such a service.

Once you have an idea of the total, the difficulty is in getting a sense of how many sessions it takes to get there, and what you might ideally charge for each session. It might be easier to think about what you think you would be worth for a day's work, and then use that to get a starting point for an hourly rate. But you shouldn't be embarrassed about putting a significant price on the skill you offer. If your work helps one man refrain from committing suicide and leaving a young family, or helps one woman stop abusing alcohol and keeps her with her partner and children, think of the financial and emotional cost that you have helped others avoid. In an ideal world, what would it be ethically reasonable for you to charge for your skill?

Second, regardless of what you think you might be worth, you must consider what you need to charge to cover your costs and make a living. Most counsellors are trained in counselling, but very few have any experience of running a business, and most are very naive about their costs. Unless what you charge covers your business running costs and your tax bill, you will never make a profit, never make enough money to earn an income of any size, and will, in effect, actually be paying people to allow you to indulge in a little hobby that gives you illusions of significance. For a fuller discussion of business running costs and earning an income, see "What are business expenses and why do I need to bother about them?".

Third, you need to be aware of what your local market could afford to pay. People in some parts of the country can generally afford to pay more than others. Some areas have higher employment rates than others and also have a greater proportion of professional people who tend to have larger amounts of disposable income to spend on therapy. Several years ago, I was on a course at a university in the Midlands. Some of the people who attended the course travelled some distance to attend. One person came from a depressed seaside resort. If you drew a line from that resort to the university city and plotted along that line what people were paying for counselling, you could see the prices go up as people lived closer to the city. At the time, clients were paying £15 a session on the coast and £40 a session in the city. Because I am willing to conduct therapy via internet video, I occasionally get clients and supervisees from London who cannot afford London prices and who are happy to work with a cheaper regional alternative.

Fourth, you might want to use your pricing as a marketing tool. You will need to be aware of what your local competitors are charging. It may be that you want to keep your charges roughly in line with theirs. It might be that you could see a commercial advantage in charging slightly less in the hope of attracting clients. Some counsellors deliberately charge more than their competitors because they believe they are worth it, and because they know that some clients are likely to choose someone with higher fees, believing they will get a better service. As advertisers know, "more expensive packaging" has an appeal for some.

Fifth, you might want to use your pricing as a control tool. I know of one therapist who charges more for evening appointments than for daytime ones. This encourages clients to think hard about whether they could come in the daytime. It effectively says: "If you want to come in the evening, I will expect you to pay me more because I am working unsocial hours." Some counsellors who have more demand for their service than they can cope with (yes, it does actually happen) start to charge more to reduce the demand for their services. Some counsellors who want to cut down as they approach retirement charge more as a way of reducing their workload.

The sixth factor is the amount of income you wish to earn or think you could reasonably earn. If you want an arguably modest annual turnover (not profit) of £25,000, you will have to have a lot of clients, week-in, week-out. However, if you charge £50 a session, you would need to see 500 clients (approximately only 10 a week). But if you charged only £25, you would need to see 1,000 clients (approximately 20 a week). See "How much can I expect to earn?".

The advantage of working in private practice is that you are free to both make and change decisions. You could charge different prices over a period of time and monitor how this affects the number of client sessions and therefore your income. You don't have to decide on one figure and then stick with it regardless of the effect.

CHAPTER EIGHT

How much can I expect to earn?*

I once knew a lady who ran an informal ironing service. Friends would drop off items of clothing to her at the start of the day and she would return them, ironed, to their homes, at the end of the afternoon. At the time, she was charging £0.35 per garment, and she felt she was earning a little "pin money". When she had more time on her hands, she wanted to turn the service into a more formal business. We had sat down and calculated her legitimate business expenses (for example, insurance, electricity, equipment, telephone, transport, national insurance) and looked at the number of garments she could realistically expect to iron in a year. It soon became apparent that if you divided her total running costs by the number of garments she would expect to iron, she needed to charge at least £1 if she stood any chance of beginning to make a profit. She decided she could never

*A version of this material originally appeared in Rye, J. (2011). Adding it up. *The Independent Practitioner,* Autumn: 6–9. Used with BACP's kind permission.

charge £1, continued to charge £0.35, continued to pay her business running costs, and told herself that she was making a little money, even though in reality she was losing a lot. Income does not equal profit.

We will look at business costs in more detail in "What are business expenses and why do I need to bother about them?". All counselling businesses, even those run from home, will have significant expenditure. It will cost you money to provide a service. There are expenses associated with the room, with communication, with insurance, with post-qualification training, supervision and other professional fees, possible transport costs. Unless your income exceeds what it costs you to offer your service, you will not make a profit. However, not all counsellors know what it costs them to run their business.

In order to help counsellors begin to get an idea of how much they might earn, I have produced Table 1, below. In order to appreciate what the numbers mean, you need to take on board the following:

For illustration purposes, I have assumed that it costs £6,300 to run the business (for example, expenses associated with things such as room hire, professional fees, training, communication, accountancy). Your business expenses might be a lot more or a lot less, but the premise behind the numbers in the table is that it costs £6,300 to run the business. Included in this figure is a guestimate of £3,000 room hire charge.

The top row gives the desired income that you might want to have. This is income after expenses and before tax. So, in order to have, for example, an income of £25,000, you would need to have a turnover of £31,300 (£25,000 plus £6,300). You would probably be taxed on that £25,000, and depending on your business structure (see "What is the difference between a sole

Table 1. Average number of paid weekly therapy sessions needed to generate desired income (after business expenses of £6,300).

Desired income £1,000	5	10	15	20	25	30	35	40	45	50
Session rate										
£20	12	17	23							
£25	10	14	18	22						
£30	8	12	15	19	22					
£35	7	10	13	16	19	22	25			
£40	6	9	11	14	17	19	22	25		
£45	5	8	10	12	15	17	20	22	24	
£50	5	7	9	11	13	15	18	20	22	24
£55	4	6	8	10	12	14	16	18	20	22
£60	4	6	8	9	11	13	15	16	18	20
£65	4	5	7	9	10	12	14	15	17	18
£70	3	5	6	8	10	11	13	14	16	17
£75	3	5	6	7	9	10	12	13	15	16

trader and a limited company?"), and your personal financial situation, you might end up with something like £20,000.

The figures in the table give the number of paid session rates you would need to have each week to achieve the desired income figure. So, if you wanted an income of £10,000 and charged £40, you would need to have nine paid sessions each week. If you wanted an income of £35,000 and charged £60, you would need to have fifteen paid sessions each week.

Please note two important facts. First, the figures in the table have been calculated assuming a forty-eight-week working year. If you want longer holidays, you would need to increase the number of paid hours. Second, the paid hours have to be maintained each week over the whole year (or at least average out at the number in the table). All of us can have the odd busy week. If we are to run a business that generates a significant income (and I fully accept that not all therapists want to do that), then we need to have the relevant number of paid sessions week-in and week-out.

If you wish to generate a significant income, you will need a regular supply of clients in reasonable numbers each week. If you are to achieve this, it is doubtful that you can gain such numbers merely by sitting and waiting for them to arrive. You will need to take marketing, having different income streams, and working for EAPs seriously, and develop skills and commitment in these areas in addition to having your therapeutic expertise. Generating an income requires developing business skills as well as therapeutic ones.

CHAPTER NINE

How can I accept payment?

In one sense, the answer to this question is very obvious. Most therapists accept cash or cheques. However, cash and cheques are "old technology" and are sometimes the least convenient for clients. Businesses looking to the future, and looking to make payment as easy as possible for people, will want to seriously consider other options.

Cash

Cash payments can be immediate. However, if you charge something like £35 or £48 per session, make sure that you have a supply of change available as clients will inevitably give you four or five £10 notes.

Because, in the eyes of some, cash payments can have an air of "he or she is trying to avoid paying tax and this cash income will not be declared on tax returns", make sure that you receipt the cash payments and record them in your accounts.

Cheque

Although I accept payment by cheque, I inwardly groan every time that I do. This is because:

- Cheques are expensive. I have to pay business bank charges for their deposit.
- Cheques take up time. I don't live near a bank and deposit mine via post. I have to complete deposit slips, put stamps on the envelope (more expense), and walk to the post box.
- Cheques can contain errors, and as banks charge for returning cheques, this can also be very expensive. People can misspell the payee name, get the date seriously wrong, put in an incorrect amount, or forget to sign. All these things have to be carefully checked, and if I fail to do it at the time and notice the mistake later, then I have to contact the client and arrange for another cheque to be sent to me. And of course, with cheques, there is always the possibility that clients may not have enough money in their accounts to honour the payment.

Bank transfer

Fortunately, as people become more comfortable with online banking, this method of payment is becoming more popular. Clients can easily and quickly transfer money into your account, and it doesn't cost you or the client anything. By checking your online bank account on a daily basis, it is easy to see how much money has or hasn't been paid into your account. If you are to offer therapy in any context other than face to face, the ability to receive money quickly over distance is important, and bank transfer is just one way of doing this. And, of course, most EAPs and companies and other agencies will want to pay by bank transfer. In the last financial year, over fifty per cent of payments into my business have been by bank transfer.

Mobile phone payment (PayM)

It is now possible to receive payments into your registered bank account from clients who send a payment from their account to your mobile number. The system is currently free, though charges may be introduced later. All you have to do is register your mobile phone number with your bank and let them know which account you want any money paid into. For full details, see http://www.paym.co.uk. The advantage of this is that it makes making a payment as easy as sending a text, and the client can do it in your presence at the end of a session (like handing over cash or a cheque), or from a distance.

Credit/debit card

Many clients would prefer to pay by card. It is quick and easy, and it is a technology they are familiar with. It saves finding the cheque book and writing a cheque, and means they don't have to go to the cash machine before the session. In a recent survey (BACP News, *Therapy Today*, March 2016, p.43), it was clear that, although relatively few counsellors accepted card payments, many of them reported they probably would if they could find an effective way of doing so.

Years ago, there were significant costs and several difficulties involved in taking card payments.

These made it virtually impossible (and certainly not cost-effective) for small businesses to do so. You had to have a merchant account with a bank. You had to pay a considerable sum for the card reader. You had to have a minimum monthly card payment turnover. You had to pay a monthly rental for the service. And you had to pay transaction charges as well. Fortunately, most of those difficulties and many of the costs have disappeared. There are now at least two ways of accepting card payments.

PayPal

Any business can open a PayPal business account (free). Once you have a PayPal account, you can use the invoicing facilities within the account to send either an email, or a formal invoice requesting money, to anyone with an email address. That email comes with a weblink which takes the recipient to a secure payment page. If the recipients have a PayPal account, they can simply pay using their own PayPal account. However, if they don't have a PayPal account, they can pay using their own debit or credit card (and they do not have to sign up to open a PayPal account). There are no monthly rental fees. As the person requesting the money, you pay a small transaction charge once the money is paid (approximately three per cent).

Chip and pin reader

Several companies (see, for example, Payleven—http://www.payleven.com) now offer businesses the option of purchasing a chip and pin card reader (costing around £50, but the prices are dropping). With many of them, there is no minimum monthly transaction requirement, and no monthly rental fee. The chip and pin readers are usually controlled by an app on your smartphone. You use your phone to enter an amount, hand the reader to the client, who inserts their card and enters their pin number. Once the transaction is approved, payment is taken and a receipt can be issued. Each transaction costs you a small fee (approximately three per cent). Once you have a history with the company, you can apply to Payleven to be able to take card payments over the phone without the user being present (you enter the details on a secure screen) just like when you purchase something over the phone using your card.

I have found the ability to take card payments to be extremely important in my business. Currently around twenty-five per cent of my income is received using credit/debit cards, and I can only see that percentage increasing. The cost of the reader and the transaction fees are recorded as a legitimate business expense to be set against tax, and in my view, are worth it in terms of providing clients with an easy way of paying me. I use both of the above in the following ways:

- taking payments from clients who want to pay by card, or who have forgotten to bring cash or cheque with them, but have cards (Payleven reader), or who ask me to send them an invoice with a card payment link (PayPal account);
- taking payments from phone or Skype clients (Payleven client not present service, or PayPal invoice);
- taking payments from clients who book for my training days:

- by putting a PayPal payment link for card payments on the website
- or by invoicing them with a PayPal payment link
- or by taking payments over the phone using my Payleven account from clients who prefer not to use their credit card on the internet.

CHAPTER TEN

Should I give the first session for free?

Reasons for doing so

Some therapists offer clients a free first session. There are at least two possible reasons why they might do this.

First, for some, it might be done as a matter of principle. Some counsellors feel that assessment is a vital part of any therapeutic relationship and they want to spend time doing an assessment thoroughly. They feel that at this stage there has been no commitment on either side for the two parties to work together and therefore it would be wrong to take money for that.

Second, some might do it as a marketing ploy. Given that, broadly speaking, there are too many counsellors "chasing" too few clients, anything that gives a counsellor a distinctive edge is attractive. Also, because counselling isn't usually cheap, anything that reduces the overall cost of therapy is likely to appeal to some clients. Most counsellors know that clients often experience considerable stress around attending the first session. A free first session might help motivate the clients to come. Once clients have overcome the hurdle of the first session, they are likely to continue to come, and from a business perspective, that is where counsellors will get their income. For some, it is worth losing the first session fee in order to gain income from the many other sessions attended.

Some therapists acknowledge that the first session is usually different in some way and charge a reduced fee for the first session, or charge the same fee but extend the time of the first session, giving time for a longish assessment to be completed. It may not be free, but it is still "giving" the client something in this session.

Reasons for not doing so

Despite good reasons for not charging for the first session, there are counter-arguments.

Some argue that there is a greater pressure to move towards doing some therapeutic work in a first session in private practice than there is in some other contexts. People do not usually arrive at the private practitioner's door with sacks of money saying, "I have thousands of pounds to spend on counselling, so take as long as you want." In their minds, they usually have a much smaller sum that they are willing to spend, and they want to feel that they are getting value. The first session is important, and because of this, many therapists would want the client to get something from it other than being asked a lot of questions. Many private practitioners will choose to do their assessments informally over a few sessions while at the same time beginning to work with the client. Some practitioners (those using a solution-focused approach, for example) will not do any assessment, believing that any encouragement for the client to repeat their "bad story" is likely to be counter-productive. The point is that many therapists are doing therapeutic work in the first session and see no reason why they shouldn't charge for that work.

But supposing that all that was happening in the first session is an assessment, why shouldn't the therapist charge for that? The client is buying the therapist's time and professional skill and knowledge. Many other professions would charge three-figure sums for an assessment and justify the amount by pointing to the time spent and to their years of training and experience and development of their professional skills. And there are business costs associated with that hour of time. Why should counsellors feel embarrassed about charging for an hour of their time during which "all" they did was an assessment?

Other counsellors would also have moral qualms about offering a first session free. They would feel uncomfortable about using money to attract clients and feel that if clients are to come to counselling, they should want to come strongly enough to arrive without financial inducements having to be used.

From a business perspective, consider the costs. If you normally charge a fee of £40 per session and work for 48 weeks a year, and if you then do not charge for two first sessions a week (not an unreasonable number in a busy practice), you would theoretically be turning your back on £3,840 ($2 \times 40 \times 48$) worth of income. That is a considerable amount of money that most therapists could not afford to ignore.

You decide

If you feel uncomfortable about charging for the first session, but can feel the force of the arguments for doing so, at least one possible compromise solution is available. I know of one therapist who partially lets the client decide. Either before the first session when the appointment is fixed (by phone, for example), or at the very beginning of the first session itself, he explains something like the following: "This first session is exploratory for both of us. It is about me working out whether or not it would be appropriate for me to work with you, and for you to work out whether you can work with me. If at the end of the session, I felt that it would be inappropriate for me to work with you, I would explain why and offer to refer you to another colleague, and I would not charge for this session. Alternatively, if you felt you couldn't work with me for any reason, I would also not charge for this session. However, if we both feel we could work together and you book a second appointment, I would like to charge for this session and all subsequent ones."

You have to decide for yourself where you stand on this issue. Practice varies considerably in the profession. There is no right answer.

CHAPTER ELEVEN

Should I charge for sessions when a client doesn't turn up or cancels with short notice?

I'm afraid that the experience of many private practitioners is that clients sometimes don't turn up or don't give 24 hours' notice of any cancellation. A rough guesstimate from looking back over my diary and from talking informally to private practitioner friends would suggest that this happens between ten and twenty per cent of the time. If you have a twenty-session week booked, you could expect *at least* four of those appointments not to happen.

If just one client a week fails to arrive, and if you receive no money for that slot, that represents an annual income loss of £1,920 (based on £40 session fee and a forty-eight-week working year). Regardless of the loss of profit in your pocket, if that money were to be invested in your business, it could have more than paid for your accountant, or easily enabled you to upgrade your computer system, and still left you with spare cash.

And of course, it isn't that simple. For private practitioners who work outside of their homes and hire premises, there are outgoings that have to be paid for. If the client doesn't arrive, or if the client doesn't cancel in sufficient time to enable you to fill the relevant diary slot, you will have incurred travel and possibly parking costs, as well as charges for the use of the room. You will have spent out for that hour and received no income to cover it.

Reasons for non-attendance or insufficient cancellation

There are a variety of reasons for filled appointment slots being left empty.

- Clients forget. On a good day it can happen to all of us. However, many clients are having a series of bad days and are experiencing emotional upheaval and chaos. Forgetfulness is a classic symptom of stress. Occasionally it just happens.
- Clients can't afford to keep coming. Our fees may be legitimate, but they represent a substantial outgoing to someone on, or just above, minimum wage. A sudden demand for spare cash might mean there is none left for the appointment, and it is too embarrassing (and expensive) to come and say so.
- Clients decide they don't want to come. If it is a first appointment, they may have lost their nerve, changed their mind, or found alternative solutions (or found someone cheaper). (See "How can I increase the chances of an enquiry becoming a client?" for ways of helping ensure that first appointments happen.) If it isn't a first appointment, clients may be dissatisfied with the therapy and vote with their feet, or it may just be that they feel they have done enough for the time being. Because of our training,

we want things to be neat and have proper endings, but sometimes they just don't happen.

- Clients experience sudden changes in their circumstances. An employer might suddenly require the client to work extra hours, or a client's partner might suddenly be required to work, so that the client has to look after children at short notice. There might be a sudden medical emergency for the client or in the client's close family. One of my own clients once failed to arrive because she was involved in a road accident on the journey to me.

To charge or not to charge

Some counsellors insist on charging for all sessions missed without inadequate notice. They argue that that agreement has been part of their written contract with the client and its enforcement is a necessary part of keeping a boundary. Some even insist on pre-payment for one or more sessions as a way of guaranteeing receipt of income for any missed or late-cancelled session.

I take a less rigid view. In my written contract with clients, I state that I *reserve the right to charge* a full fee for missed or late-cancelled appointments (i.e., that I will make a decision about each case) rather than that I will automatically do so. I think that *always* charging for missed or late-cancelled appointments is often unfair and usually unproductive.

Certainly, it seems unfair to do anything that you have not told clients about, so however you decide to proceed, you must state that in your contract. However, I personally feel it is unfair to charge clients for missed or late-cancelled appointments due to circumstances beyond their control. I once missed a supervision appointment because I had to rush to the accident and emergency department of my local hospital to be with my wife who had been involved in an accident. I know I would have thought it extremely unfair if my supervisor had then imposed a financial penalty on me for my failure to attend my appointment with her.

I have seen it argued that if you don't charge on every occasion, regardless of circumstances, that this somehow changes your relationship. Some people think it somehow makes it less professional, that you are treating the client like a friend. I personally disagree with this. If I return goods to a shop and expect a refund, I fully understand that in many shops the customer service department will make an individual judgement about the worthiness of my request, and that in some cases I would get it, and in others not. It is not about the shop wanting to be my friend. It is about the shop making financial reparation based on a judgement of the worthiness of my case.

I fully understand the arguments about the need to help clients be responsible for their own therapy and about the need to not let clients financially abuse the therapist. However, whenever I have felt it fair and have charged for missed or late-cancelled sessions, although it may have made a professional point that the client may (or may not) have understood, it has only very rarely produced money. The clients who have decided to end by not turning up don't re-book, and certainly don't respond to reasonable requests for payment. And the clients who may have thought of continuing their therapy despite a missed or unreasonably late-cancelled session usually decide to finish when that session is charged for, thus causing the therapist to lose future income as well as present loss. Making the point to the client may be therapeutically necessary and beneficial to them, but it may arguably financially shoot the therapist in the foot. So, I don't charge for missed or late-cancelled sessions on every occasion, and when I do decide to do so, I am not overly optimistic about the outcome.

"But what about my loss of income and my room expenses?" I hear you cry. Well, as I have argued, in my experience (yours may be different), charging is unlikely to generate the lost income. I think that income lost from these appointments and the outgoings are just part of my business overheads. I can make any fair and reasonable attempts to reduce them, but their reality is one of the factors I need to take into account when calculating my session fees. The fees for those who do attend or give fair notice of cancellation will sadly have to be higher to cover the financial losses incurred from those who don't.

Advance payment

One way of getting over the problems of non-payment for late cancellations or non-attendance is by asking for payment in advance. Some counsellors ask clients to pay for a number of sessions in advance (say, for example, six). Others just ask for a deposit of the fee for one session in advance, so on the first meeting they pay for two sessions and, if they attend all sessions as arranged, get their last session "free" (having already paid for it at the first meeting).

If you have moderately wealthy clients, I can see that this might work. However, I spend a lot of time and effort in trying to get clients and in reducing the number of hurdles they have to face in coming to me. I personally don't charge in advance (and arguably pay the price) because I don't want that to be an off-putting hurdle that would stop some clients working with me. I might lose the odd session fee, but then arguably I gain considerably more that I otherwise wouldn't have had if they didn't come at all.

Working for EAPs and other companies

If you are offered work by an EAP or rehabilitation agency, or are approached directly by the HR department of a local company, it is important to understand what the terms are for DNAs (did not attends) and LCs (late cancellations). In my experience, those terms can vary considerably.

Some companies will pay a full or half fee for the first failed appointment and nothing after that. Some will pay full fee for the first, half fee for the second, and nothing for any subsequent failed appointments (though many would automatically close the counselling down after two failed appointments). Some companies would pay nothing at all for a failed appointment.

I was once offered some work by a local agency providing counselling for the long-term unemployed. The initial contract was to work with four clients for up to six sessions. There was no payment for failed appointments. Once the initial contract was over, I declined the offer of further work. Quite simply, it became uneconomic to do it.

What I soon realised (something I should have foreseen) was that this particular client group was likely to have a high rate of failed appointments. Some were reluctant clients who had agreed to counselling only because they feared losing benefits. Some were very depressed with chaotic lifestyles and getting up in the morning was a big enough challenge. Travelling to therapy on time was a huge ask. Some genuinely could not afford the travelling costs. Some were unemployed because of long-term illness which made travelling difficult. With this group, there were a high number of failed appointments and I ended up losing rather than making income through the contract.

Local companies who contact you directly (rather than employ the services of an EAP) usually haven't considered failed appointments. I now make it clear what my terms are. And, of course, because you are self-employed, you can vary these terms if you wish to do so. With one company, I reserve the right to charge a full fee for the first, a half fee for the second and any subsequent missed appointments. With another company with which I have a long-term relationship, and which has provided me with a large number of clients over the years, I now charge only a half fee for a failed appointment.

My experience is that working directly for local companies can be much less financially risky than working for EAPs and rehabilitation agencies. Because the counselling is arranged by the company's HR department, the client retains some sense of direct obligation to the employer and is less likely to miss or late-cancel a session.

CHAPTER TWELVE

What are business expenses, and why do I need to bother about them?

Although some of the counsellors I meet when running training days on setting up in business are reluctant to face these things, it is very important both to acknowledge that running a business involves expenditure, and to know how much that expenditure is. Running a business costs money, and if you don't know how much it costs, you can never know if you are making a profit or a loss. Income does not equal profit. If your business costs more to run than you are taking in income, you are running your business at a loss. And while it may be acceptable to make a loss for a year or two in the hope of eventually making a profit, it doesn't make any sense to go on losing money in the long term.

Some counsellors are deceived into thinking that they are making a profit by the fact that they regularly collect money from clients. If you take approximately £400 a month in counselling fees, you might be tempted to think that you are making £4,800 a year profit. But if your business expenses are £420 a month (not an unreasonable amount), you are actually making an annual loss of £240.

What are business expenses?

A business expense is an amount of money that you have needed to spend in order to conduct your business. The Inland Revenue talks about the need for your business expenses to be both "ordinary" and "necessary". An ordinary expense is one that is common and accepted in your profession or business. A necessary expense is one that is helpful and appropriate for your trade or business. Using a telephone would be an ordinary and necessary expense for counsellors, but the purchase of a set of recordings by Elvis Presley would be extremely difficult (and probably impossible) to justify for psychotherapeutic practitioners.

Because running a counselling business does not involve buying and selling large amounts of physical stock, in the way that running a book-selling business does, for example, it is easy for counsellors to think that they don't have a lot of expenses. But counsellors do have significant expenses, even if those expenses may not be as immediately obvious as a back room full of new books to sell.

It may be helpful to think of those expenses under two broad headings.

Communication and running an office expenses

- If you are to communicate with clients, you need to use a phone and possibly a mobile phone. You could pay for a separate landline and have a dedicated business mobile phone. Most people start out by designating a reasonable and realistic proportion of their phone usage as business usage and charging an appropriate proportion of their telephone bills to the business.

- If you have a business email address and website, there are domain name charges and charges associated with building, hosting, and maintaining your business website.
- You are likely to have advertising costs. Apart from any physical materials, you may have to pay fees to have your website listed in important directories (such as the BACP Directory and the Counselling Directory).
- There are general office expenses such as stationery, business cards, and postage.
- You will have business banking charges.
- If you are renting a room, you will have room hire costs, and you may have office furniture costs too.
- You may need to purchase appropriate software (Microsoft Office, Evernote, QuickBooks Accounts, for example), or you may need to rent office and accounting software from Cloud providers (Microsoft Office, KashFlow, for example).
- You may wish to use the services of a virtual personal assistant to handle your phone calls and take messages while you are with clients.
- Heating and lighting costs. If you hire a room, it should be easy to claim for these. If working from home, discuss with your accountant if you could charge an appropriate proportion of your overall heating and lighting costs to the business.
- Discuss with your accountant whether or not you can claim the full or partial cost of any equipment used wholly or significantly for the business—computers, for example.

Professional fees and personal development expenses

- Your annual membership subscription to your professional body.
- Your supervision expenses.
- You are likely to benefit from the services of an accountant.
- Your annual subscription to the Information Commissioner's Office.
- Your annual subscription to the Disclosure and Barring Update Service.
- Your professional insurance costs.
- If you work from home and/or use your own vehicle for the business, you can claim the additional cost of your home contents, building, and car insurance because of your business usage.
- Although you cannot claim your initial training costs, once qualified you can claim the costs associated with certain ongoing training.
- Professional books and journals.
- Travel, parking, and subsistence associated with certain ongoing training and supervision.

An example business

In order to bring home the point that it does cost you money for you to offer counselling to people (even though they are paying you a fee for that counselling), I want to put some figures on the headings above. However, please note that the figures in Table 2 are only illustrative. Different businesses have different expenses. Your business may cost considerably less to run; on the other hand, it may cost considerably more.

Table 2. Examples of business expenses.

Telephony costs (12 × £30)	£360
Domain name, email, and website costs (12 × £20)	£240
Advertising and directory subscriptions	£300
General office (stationery, postage)	£50
Software rental and secure cloud storage (12 × £15)	£180
Virtual personal assistant (12 × £10)	£120
Heat and light (12 × £10)	£120
Room hire (12 × £200)	£2,400
Professional fees	£200
Supervision (12 × £60)	£720
Accountant	£600
Information Commission	£40
Disclosure and Barring Service renewal	£12
Professional insurance	£90
Additional insurance costs	£100
Additional training (one big conference, one local event)	£200
Business travel @ £0.45 per mile	£70
Books	£60
Total	£5,862

If these were your business costs and you charged £45 per session, you would have to conduct 131 sessions to cover your costs before you started to make a profit; if you charged only £30, you would have to have 196 sessions before you started to make a profit. If you work from home, your costs are likely to be much smaller because you do not have room hire expense.

Two continuing professional development (CPD) events

Let's make the example above a bit more concrete by taking two counsellors going on typical CPD events. Everything they spend in relation to their business needs to be recorded and claimed.

The network meeting

Richard wants to go to a local network meeting of counsellors in a nearby city. The meeting is planned from 6:30 p.m. to 9:30 p.m. Because the event is nearly an hour's drive away and starts early, he is going to miss an evening meal unless he has one en route. He knows of a chain burger restaurant approximately half way between his home and the meeting venue.

He reaches the restaurant and has a quick burger meal and feels able to charge this expense (£4.59) as otherwise he would have had to have eaten ridiculously early or late. The meal out seemed a necessary part of him going to the meeting. He made sure he kept the receipt.

When at the meeting, he paid the event fee of £10. He drove home and made a note of the mileage (a total of 90 miles).

The expenses that Richard remembered to claim as legitimate business costs were:

Subsistence (meal)	£4.95
Event fee	£10.00
Travel (90 miles @ £0.45)	£40.50
Total	£55.45

Attending a £10 meeting in a nearby city actually cost £55.45.

The day conference

Vanita was going to attend a day conference in London. Because she lived in Leeds and the conference started at 10:00 a.m., she decided that she couldn't face getting up very early, risk being late for the start, and being too exhausted to benefit from the day. So, she would travel up the night before. This would involve her leaving her car in the station car park, and paying for overnight accommodation and an evening meal in addition to the normal conference costs. Vanita also bought three books while at the conference.

The expenses that Vanita remembered to claim as legitimate business costs were:

Parking at the station	£8
Return train ticket	£74
Underground fares	£7
Evening meal	£22
Accommodation and breakfast	£150
Conference fee (including meals)	£120
Books	£57
Total	£438

Attending a £120 conference in London actually cost £438.

Please note that in both of the above examples, it *could* be argued that the actual costs were even higher. Both counsellors lost income by attending the events. Let's assume that both counsellors charge, for example, £40 per session. It could be argued that in forgoing two evening appointments, the event cost Richard an extra £80. It could also be argued that it cost Vanita an extra £200 as she missed sessions with at least five paying clients while she was away. Please note, however, that lost income *cannot* be claimed as a legitimate business expense.

Paying less tax

The Inland Revenue requires you to keep a record of your income and expenses. This record could be physically recorded in an accounts book, or electronically stored on a spreadsheet or in an accounts program. You also need to have invoices or receipts to back up each expense you are claiming, and these accounts and documentation should be kept for at least three years.

It is extremely important to know what your legitimate business expenses are because without that information you will end up paying too much tax. You are only taxed on the amount of profit you make, and as mentioned before, income does not equal profit. Profit is what you have left over after your expenses have been taken out of your income.

It is beyond the scope of this book to give detailed tax advice. How much you should pay (if any at all) will depend on your individual circumstances and overall income, and you are encouraged to seek professional advice about your individual tax situation. The example below is for illustration purposes only, to show the need to know and record your legitimate business expenses. You need to seek financial advice about your exact tax obligations.

If, for example, you were a sole trader, and your annual business turnover was £16,000, and you had no other income, and you claimed no business expenses, you might end up paying around £900 in tax.

Income	£16,000
Govt. tax-free allowance e.g.	£11,500
Business expenses claimed	£0
Taxable income (£16,000–£11,500)	£4,500
Tax at, for example, 20%	£900
Alleged profit after tax	£15,100

Even though in the above case you haven't claimed business expenses, you have still had to spend that money to run your business. Your apparently large profit is a delusion.

However, if you were a sole trader, and your annual business turnover was £16,000, and you had no other income, and you claimed £4,000 in legitimate business expenses, you might end up paying only £100 in tax (a considerable reduction) and your smaller profit would be an accurate reflection of the truth.

Income	£16,000
Govt. tax-free allowance e.g.	£11,500
Business expenses claimed	£4,000
Taxable income (£16,000–£15,500)	£500
Tax at, for example, 20%	£100
Actual profit after tax	£11,900

Marketing

CHAPTER THIRTEEN

What are your tips for marketing my business? (1)

In order to answer this question, there are, perhaps, three other questions to ask. Why? What? Where?

Why?

If you want to catch a fish, you have to go fishing.

The need to advertise may seem obvious to some, but sadly, it isn't obvious to all. I can think of many counsellors who have started up in business who are reluctant to market themselves and who never seem to get round to it with any commitment. They then wonder why they have so few clients. Once you have an established business and a good reputation, you may be able to cut back on the advertising, but when starting out it is essential that you tell others about yourself.

Perhaps some reluctance may be caused by a natural reticence about self-promotion. It may be caused by a naïve belief that people will somehow, mysteriously suddenly start coming to you. It may be down to not knowing how to start. I suspect that a big reason is a failure on the part of therapists to fully accept that they are changing gear and running a business rather than just doing therapy ("Surely all I have to worry about is being a good counsellor? I don't really have to do this commercial stuff, do I?").

I repeat, if you want to catch a fish, you have to go fishing.

What?

We all have our pet hates, don't we—things that cause an irrational response that is disproportionate to the actual thing itself. I must come clean and reveal that one of my biggest pet hates is some of the content of advertising material that counsellors often use.

Counsellors sometimes have, *as their primary advertising message*, something vague and woolly about the counselling process as they attempt to describe this to clients. It can best be illustrated in the clause "I offer you a safe place to explore ...".

Other counsellors have, *as their primary advertising message*, something long and complicated about the multiple, strange-sounding supercalifragilisticexpialidocious qualifications that they have (talk about trying to blind someone with science): "I am a psychoanalytic, transactional, psychotherapeutic, person-centred, solution-focused, EMDR qualified, MBACP senior accredited, and registered counsellor ...". Hopefully, the person just mentioned doesn't actually exist, but you take my point.

Please don't misunderstand me. I fully accept that it is valuable, even important, to give your potential clients some idea of what the counselling process may involve, and I also agree that it is important to let clients know what your qualifications and potential areas of expertise are, but don't thrust this into their faces as the first thing you communicate.

Running a successful business involves offering people a product that they want, at a price they can afford, at a time and place that appeals to them. You need to think about the product you are offering, and make sure that it is something that clients want.

A long time ago, in another life, I used to teach a course on creative writing. A student on the course once came to me with a carrier bag full of her poems, asked me to read them, and then asked me to help her get them published. After a weekend of selective reading, I spent some time with her in the next session explaining the following:

- Very few people were reading poetry, especially poetry by unknown poets.
- Because very few people were reading poetry, hardly any publishers were publishing poetry (it wasn't worth the financial risk).
- Because of the above, she had very little chance of getting her poems published, regardless of any merit that they may, or may not, have had.
- She would stand a greater chance of getting into print if she studied what the market wanted and used her talents to produce writing that fitted that brief.

Many counsellors start with themselves and the skills they have to offer, rather than asking themselves what the market wants (what people are prepared to spend money on). I feel reasonably confident that very few (if any) potential clients wake up in the morning and say to themselves, "I want a safe place to explore ...". I feel equally confident that very few wake up and say, "I want a psychoanalytic, transactional, psychotherapeutic, person-centred, solution-focused, EMDR qualified, MBACP senior accredited, and registered counsellor ...". However, I strongly suspect that many of them do wake up and think some of the following to themselves:

- I need some help with my anger.
- I feel really low and have been feeling like this for too long.
- I just wish I could stop being so anxious.
- I am so stressed at work.
- I still feel so guilty about the termination.
- Will I ever get over this grief?
- All my relationships seem to end disastrously. Is it me?
- I haven't been able to drive since my accident, but I need to start again if I am ever to return to work.
- I need to stop gambling online before my partner leaves me.
- I can't decide whether or not to go ahead with the wedding.
- We desperately need a good couple counsellor.

My point is simple. Make sure that your material offers potential clients something that they would want to buy (expertise in helping them help themselves in relation to the above), in language they would understand, rather than offering them something you think they ought to want, in language you think they ought to understand.

Three other brief points before we move on to Where?

First, make sure that your material contains all the information the client is likely to need. For example, clients don't just wake up and think, "I need some help with my anger ...". They tend to think, "I need some help with my anger. I wonder if there is anyone good locally who offers anger management, and I wonder how much it would cost?" Giving specific information about location and cost can be important for a client when making a choice about who to select. If you miss that information off your material, you are, in effect, making it more difficult for clients to choose you.

Second, make sure that the information you give clients is honest. As part of our ethical responsibility, we should not work beyond our competence. Very few (if any) counsellors could claim to be competent in all areas—though you might be forgiven for thinking this by looking at the length of the lists of competencies in which some counsellors claim expertise. It is also important to be honest about our training and qualifications. Claiming to have expertise in CBT on the basis of a two-year part-time course run by a local university is very different from claiming the same expertise on the basis of a five-hour workshop provided by a local counselling group. We need to be careful not to give the impression that we have more competence than we have. Similarly, we might have a doctorate, but unless the subject matter was counselling (or counselling-related), choosing to use it in counselling practice publicity is clearly misleading.

Third, another part of what we have to offer clients is not just our therapeutic product (or range of products), but how we offer that material and those interactions (face to face, telephone, video, or internet chat). If we feel comfortable in offering something other than face-to-face contact, then it is important to let clients know that. An ability to have flexible access to therapy might be important, for example, for the single parent who cannot get child-minding in order to attend therapy, or for the businesswoman who has to work away from home on an unpredictable basis. Flexible modality can reduce the number of barriers that clients have to cross in order to interact with us and make us available to a bigger pool of potential clients. (See "How can I increase access to my services?".)

We have an ethical obligation to provide clients with accurate information they ought to know in advance in order to make an informed decision about the services they want to receive and about how these services will be delivered. (See *Ethical Framework*, BACP, July 2016.)

CHAPTER FOURTEEN

What are your tips for marketing my business? (2)

Where?

Whenever I talk about marketing with groups of counsellors, I ask them to imagine that they have recently inherited £200 from a deceased relative, and to decide how to use this money to advertise their business. I then put them into small groups and ask them how they would spend their money. In the plenary feedback, we list multiple ways of spending the inheritance. After a while, I stop them and ask this question: "If you were a potential client and were looking for a therapist, where is the first place you would look for information?" The answer they give is always unanimous and crystal clear: "The internet!" Despite the clarity of the answer, few, if any of them, ever suggest using the money to get a website. I would argue that *the* best place to put your marketing material is on a suitable website. (See "How can I get a website?".)

Over the years, I have found one of the best ways of making a decision about whether or not to spend money on advertising in a particular place is to ask myself a question similar to the one above: "If I wanted a counsellor, would I look in this particular place to find out details of one?" If the answer is "No", I know that spending money for that particular advertising space is probably going to be a waste.

Be particularly cautious about ...

* Companies offering to put your cards into supermarkets so that customers and supermarket staff can get a small discount when they come to you and produce the card. I once paid a lot of money to have my small business cards placed on a display of cards at the end of checkouts in the local branch of a well-known supermarket. I was assured by the salesman (who, of course, had to do the deal on that day—I was very naïve then) that I would get hundreds of customers and supermarket staff coming to me for counselling. I used to go into the supermarket occasionally to check that the cards were there. After seven years, I can honestly say that I never received a single client via that route. I realise now that having paid for your shopping, you usually stagger out of the store and don't really have any interest in perusing the tiny business cards of local services. It is not something that I would do myself, so why should I expect others to do it?
* Phone calls from GP surgeries, dentists, and hospitals asking if you want to advertise your practice on the reverse of the appointment cards that they give to their patients. Initially, I used to be very flattered by the calls ("people connected with legitimate health services actually know that I exist") until I realised that marketing companies were just working down lists of local businesses. Such advertising may

be useful in helping keep the name of your company before people so that they might remember it and turn to you at a later date. However, although well-meaning people may think that everyone in a medical crisis needs counselling, my view is that they might need crisis support and may not yet be ready for counselling. The crisis may be too close. And again, my view is that even if I wanted a counsellor and had the name of a counsellor from an appointment card, I would still check out the internet to consider other possible options.

- Phone calls asking you if the services you offer would be of interest to teachers, or nurses, or police officers, or fire officers. The question is designed to hook you because you invariably answer, "Yes". And if the question is prefaced by something like, "I am calling on behalf of an organisation that represents thousands of police officers ...", you tend to sit up and take notice. I have had many of these calls over the years and now find them particularly distasteful. Stage one is to get you to admit that your work is relevant to this group of people. Stage two is to ask you if you would like to put details of your work before thousands of teachers/nurses/police officers/ fire officers. Once you have said yes, it then slowly emerges that you will have to pay several hundred pounds to write, what is basically an advertisement, to appear in a dedicated professional magazine going to one of the above services. I have never used these outlets because I dislike the dishonesty of the "trap" and because I'm not sure how many people would actually see the advertisement and then follow through with a booking. But, the main reason is that all of the above professions would have free access to counselling via their employee assistance programmes (see "What about working for agencies?"). Very few people would want to pay for counselling if they knew they could get it for free via work.

- Seemingly persuasive telephone calls from *Yellow Pages* telling you that their website is getting thousands of enquiries for counselling in your area and that you need to pay hundreds of pounds to get your details on their website. My problem with this is that when people use the internet to search for counsellors they rarely specifically search the *Yellow Pages* site deliberately. In my view, you would be far better to invest the money in getting a good website of your own.

Other options

- Counsellors often think it is a good idea to write letters of introduction to local GPs, practice managers, and solicitors, for example. This may be useful in certain cases. However, we all know that an unsolicited letter, when received in a pile of other more pressing ones, soon gets binned. There is also the difficulty that other professionals cannot officially refer people to you because of the risk (they might get sued if you are incompetent) and because of official commissioning processes. However, personal contact can be very useful. I regularly get private clients who have been informally told of my existence by two GPs who originally came to me as clients themselves. And when clients come to me because they have been encouraged to have counselling, but who don't want to wait for the NHS service, I always give them a business card in case they might want to take one back to their GP.

- You may feel it worth your while to consider advertising in local print outlets. Free local newspapers usually contain adverts for local services. My view is that if you advertise here, you need to do it regularly and not just as a "one off" so that readers become aware of your name. Parish magazines are another source of printed advertising, and their rates may be cheaper than local newspapers, though obviously their distribution is smaller.

- Printed directories. In addition to the *Thompson* and *Yellow Pages* directories, many areas have a local directory of services. Although most directories will try to persuade you to pay to have a larger entry, they will usually give you a basic entry for free.

- Online directories. There are seemingly countless online directories offering to include your details, and again, most of them asking for payment for a larger entry. If you are going to spend money, it might be worth thinking about which ones are likely to get you most hits. I suspect that the BACP online directory (http://www.itsgoodtotalk.org.uk/) has a lot of users who need to be able to trust the quality of the people listed (for example, solicitors, insurance companies, EAPs, rehabilitation agencies) as well as the general public. The Counselling Directory (http://www.counselling-directory.org.uk/) is site popular with many counsellors because of its flexibility, and the fact that its entries usually come high in Google searches, and it is relatively easily to try it out because you can choose to pay only for a short period. At the time of writing, PlusGuidance (http://www.plusguidance.com/) is a free online directory where you can offer face-to-face counselling as well as secure web-based sessions.

- Information sessions. One of the best ways of getting free publicity is to offer free information to people. Local newspapers will charge you to advertise, but they may be willing to run an article for free on grief following a local tragedy, for example, or report on a group that you are running on stress reduction for local business people. There are also likely to be many groups in the area that are always keen to have a speaker. If you write to them offering to come and talk about something relevant—such as stress, anger, anxiety, grief, addiction—you may find some of them willing to take you up. Of course, the purpose of the written or spoken information sessions is not to directly promote your business, but indirectly you are giving your services a free public platform.
- Social media. It is possible to set up free accounts on social media (for example, Twitter, Facebook, LinkedIn), and use them for your business. Clearly, there are ethical considerations to be taken into account when using social media, especially if you are using a personal account. However, there are at least two ways of using separate accounts for your business.

One way is to make the occasional posting advertising particular services or events ("Too worried about something? Why not book an appointment with MyCounselling? Find out more at mycounselling. biz." "Anger Management Training for Counsellors. This Venue. This Date. More details at mycounselling.biz/anger"). I have certainly picked up at least one client this way and have had a few extra people attend my training events as a result.

A second way of using social media is to regularly (say weekly or fortnightly) make professional postings on therapy-related topics in order to keep bringing your name before people and offer them useful or thought-provoking contributions. If you can create the time to do this, it may help enhance your reputation and credibility.

Don't forget to monitor the effectiveness of your advertising. When potential clients contact me, I always ask where they heard about me.

CHAPTER FIFTEEN

What else can I do to help my business grow?

If you consistently provide a quality, professional service, your positive reputation will spread, and your business will grow. You will start to get clients who have been recommended by former clients. And former clients themselves will possibly return with new issues.

And if you have a strong web presence, people will easily find you. EAPS, rehabilitation agencies, and local companies will recruit you as an affiliate and start to regularly send you referrals. Your turnover will steadily start to increase.

For some counsellors, especially those who have a second income, or those who are not depending on their business for their livelihoods, such slow growth may be enough. They may have moved from getting two clients a week to routinely getting six, and feel content. However, the reality for others is that they need a bigger income, and need to regularly achieve the equivalent of between fifteen and twenty-five (see "How much can I expect to earn?").

The problem is that there are likely to be several other counsellors in your area all competing for the same clients. So, how could you offer something different to increase the likelihood of getting a bigger proportion of those clients? And how else could your business earn money? Any answer to these questions will probably involve a medium-term plan and possibly some financial investment. When thinking about your professional development needs, think of which skills you might need that could increase your income as well as what you need immediately to improve your work with clients. For example, researching and committing to undertake, at some stage, a two-year, part-time course on clinical supervision is likely to secure more income for your business as well as develop your personal skills.

Specialisation

If you go on a marketing course, you are likely to be asked to spend some time identifying your USP—your unique selling point. If you are serious about growing your business, you do need to identify either what your unique selling points are at the moment, or what they could be in the near future.

Many counsellors come into the profession with an interest in a particular area. This interest could have come about randomly (they just found they were particularly interested in eating disorders), or it could have come from a life experience (they grew up in a family with a depressed parent), or it could have come about as a result of previous career expertise (they worked as a teacher and wanted to work therapeutically with children). In the medium term, it is worth thinking about how you could do further training, and develop this interest into a particular specialism that you offer.

It would be one way of distinguishing you from your rivals and enabling you to develop a unique selling point. That doesn't mean that you would stop offering general counselling, but rather that you would gain a reputation in your area (and perhaps nationally) as having a particular expertise, and this would increase your likelihood of getting extra clients.

For example, I have known counsellors who have developed a specialism in:

- working with bereaved clients after initially volunteering with CRUSE;
- working with anxiety after realising that many of his clients presented with anxiety issues;
- working with anger after getting a stream of requests to run anger-management sessions;
- working with mental health issues in children, after being an ex-teacher and realising that current child and adolescent mental health services were seriously under-resourced and that there was a *huge* demand for such services;
- working with personality disorders after her time working for the prison service;
- working with a particular faith group, after being brought up in that community;
- working with domestic violence after having had a career in social services dealing with similar issues;
- working with addiction issues, following his own successful struggles with alcohol;
- working with gays and lesbians because of her own sexuality;
- offering a particular type of therapy because of increasing demand for this from GPs, EAPs, and rehabilitation agencies—such as EMDR, CBT, solution-focused brief therapy.

Think about which aspect of counselling interests you and what you might be interested in developing as a specialism. Start to research any further training in this area that you might need to undertake. Make a list of five books on the topic that you could read to test out your interest and enthusiasm for the area.

Increased income streams

In a corner shop, an income stream is a category of goods that brings in money. So in a typical newsagent's, you might have the following income streams: newspapers and magazines, cigarettes, alcohol, confectionery, general groceries. When you start up your therapy business, your main (and only) income stream is likely to be general counselling. If you can think of more services you can offer, you can increase your income streams, and hence, increase the financial success of the business. If demand for income from one source slackens off, you may be able to maintain some income from other streams.

To some extent, increasing income streams overlaps with specialisation. A specialist offering (such as couple counselling) would also become another income stream. Both specialisation and increasing income streams are likely to require deliberate medium-term planning, and some additional training (and therefore extra financial investment in the business).

If you are able to undertake appropriate training, or have the relevant qualifications and/or experience, in the longer term, as your business grows, you might be able to develop some of the following income streams:

- couple counselling
- counsellor supervision

- supervising counsellors working with children
- running support groups (on anxiety, for example)
- running CPD events
- selling material for clients that you have written and self-published
- selling CPD training material that you have written and self-published for other counsellors
- offering counselling to a wider market than your immediate local one (see below).

Increased access

This may not be appropriate for all therapists, but for some, thinking about how to offer therapy to a wider audience via telephone and the internet is likely to increase their number of clients (provided they have a strong web presence so that the clients can find them).

The historical counselling model has been that you see clients in a regular time-slot, face to face, for an extended number of sessions. Increasingly, some clients are expecting more flexibility. Many of them are accessing services via telephone and the web and are willing to access a form of therapy that way too. Of course, it would not be the same as extended face-to-face therapy, and, of course, there are problems associated with it, but telephone and internet therapy are just different from face-to-face therapy, and different is just different.

For those therapists willing to do the training, think about the differences, and overcome the difficulties, they are able to access clients from across the UK, and from around the globe (and there are many ex-pats wanting a therapist). Such therapists are still fishing for clients in a pond, but the point is it is a considerably bigger pond with many, many more fish. (See "How can I increase access to my services?".)

Putting it together

When you start out, one hundred per cent of your income is likely to come from general counselling. The figures below illustrate what the proportions of your income might look like in a mature and flexible business that has followed the advice in this chapter:

Face-to-face individual general counselling	40%
Face-to-face couple counselling	3%
Telephone individual counselling	15%
Individual specialist anxiety counselling	12%
Face-to-face individual supervision	5%
Group face-to-face supervision	2%
Telephone individual supervision	4%
Internet individual supervision	5%
Training	12%
Sale of client materials	2%

You can see from the above figures that the therapist has developed a specialism, has trained to offer more than one income stream, and has increased her access to clients. As a result, less than half of her income now comes from traditional face-to-face general counselling (which is how she started out).

Other practical issues

CHAPTER SIXTEEN

What can I do to increase my personal safety when working alone?

A male counsellor had a first session with a new female client. He was alone and working from home in the evening. He went to the front door to greet her and guided her through the hallway to the counselling room. Before sitting down, she held out her hand to him and offered him something. He was surprised, but assumed she was keen to pay and was offering the session fee they had agreed over the telephone. In fact, what she was handing the man was his house keys which she had picked up on the way through the hallway. She looked at him rather sternly and said: "If you are going to invite strangers into your house, don't leave any keys on the sideboard by the front door!" He discovered during that session that she worked as a professional escort and had a lot of knowledge about, and experience of, how to keep safe when working with strangers at home.

It may be helpful to think of personal safety under three broad headings: initial screening, avoiding misunderstanding, and further practical steps to enhance safety.

Initial screening

As a therapist in private practice, it is important to remember that you are under no obligation to accept anybody as a client. You can always say "No" and refer on to other counsellors. You can make some sensible moves to make yourself safe by trying to minimise risk and refusing to take on certain clients. Depending on how vulnerable you felt, you might, for example, make a decision at the beginning of your career not to work with clients who declare that they have certain personality disorders, or you might not feel comfortable working with clients who have addictions or extreme anger issues. If you rent a room in a relatively isolated location, you might choose to have a rule, for example, that you won't work with clients after dark or at other times of particular vulnerability.

If you have a policy where you are clear that you are not necessarily going to accept nearly every client who makes an enquiry, then two important things flow from that decision. First, you need to make it plain to clients right from the beginning that any agreed early contact will be an assessment, and that you may, after the assessment, decide that it is not appropriate for you to work together, and that you may refer on to another therapist. (Obviously, because of your professional commitment to work ethically and within the bounds of your competence, you may refer certain clients on for reasons other than safety. However, if safety may be an issue, it is important to be clear about the possibility of onward referral straight away.) Second, you need a way of conducting that assessment safely. Do you do it face to face or use technology as a safety barrier? It may not suit you and may not be necessary in your situation, but a few therapists conduct the initial assessment via teleconference or telephone as a way of initially protecting their physical personal space.

Of course, not all clients who may pose a threat show that potential at a first meeting. A further way of reducing risk is to build yourself a professional escape route out of the therapy should you ever feel the need to take it. You can do this by having an extended assessment period, say, six sessions. At the beginning, you tell the client that up to six sessions may be an assessment when you are trying to work out whether it would be appropriate for you to work together and to see if you could develop a therapeutic relationship. Of course, if you felt at risk, you could always end the therapy at any point. However, consciously and clearly building and signposting regular possible exit points is likely to cause less offence if that route ever has to be taken.

Avoiding misunderstanding

Misunderstanding can cause conflict and be a source of risk, so anything that you can do to avoid misunderstanding increases safety. Transparency about any assessment process (see above) is essential. However, it is possible for misunderstanding to arise over a host of other issues: confidentiality (and under what conditions it would be broken), what counselling is and isn't, fees, payment terms, what happens if sessions are missed, length of sessions, what notes (if any) are kept, how and where they are stored, what access the client has to notes, what contact is permitted between sessions. It is extremely helpful if you have some form of signed written agreement (see "Do I have to give a written contract?") that you have talked through with the client at an early stage of the relationship. It can be useful to have something physical to refer back to to help dissipate any disagreement.

A big source of potential misunderstanding concerns what counselling is and isn't. More clients than years ago are presenting with a self-diagnosis gained from looking up their "symptoms" on the internet, or from being told by their doctor to try counselling. They come with a tendency to have a "medical" view of counselling, expecting to be able to have their symptoms further diagnosed and fixed by an expert who may have "psych" as part of her or his title. If this is the case, it can be important early on to educate clients about the process of counselling and the importance of their own work in the process.

Further possible practical steps

- Have a very loud personal alarm—hidden, but easily available. These can be purchased relatively cheaply. Alternatively, consider installing one of the many available panic button alert apps on your SmartPhone. The HollieGuard app (http://hollieguard.com/) offers an impressive array of safety options for lone workers; options that you can set to suit your particular situation.

- Make sure you understand how to use any speed dial facility on your phone and have 999 on speed dial so that you can ring the emergency services by pressing only one key.

- Do not leave keys to your door in the door, or in any other visible place.

- Think carefully about where you position your chair in relation to the door of your counselling room. It may be common practice to have the client's chair nearest the door to help them feel safe and not "trapped" by the therapist. However, with certain clients you may decide to place yourself nearest the door (to facilitate a quick escape), with the client further away in the room.

- Do not wear any neck jewellery that could be grabbed to restrain you.

- Consider refusing to book appointments with some clients at times or in locations where you feel especially vulnerable.

- Consider operating a buddy system—having someone you can call if necessary. As well as this, consider having a system whereby you routinely call your buddy at the beginning or end (or both) of a particular client's sessions so that a failure to call generates an agreed action on your buddy's part. Consider working with your buddy on a coded message system so that your client won't necessarily be wrongly alerted by any emergency phone call that you make.

    You to buddy: "Hello. Please can you cancel my appointment later. I won't be able to make it."
    Buddy to you: "Do you need assistance now?"
    You to buddy: "Yes."

- Have a clear plan in place for what you would do in the event of threat or danger. Inform your buddy/family of that plan. Rehearse that plan.

- Get an honest friend to review your non-verbal messages. Don't give off ambiguous signals or use aggressive body language.

- Don't be afraid to give short or long notice of termination (with a recommendation to another counsellor, and a return of fee if appropriate).

- Consider attending some conflict resolution training or self-defence training if appropriate.

CHAPTER SEVENTEEN

Do I need to give clients a written contract?

You may not feel the need to give clients a written contract. However, there are compelling reasons for doing so.

Private practitioners are isolated

Although upheld complaints against counsellors are comparatively few, private practitioners risk generating a disproportionate number of those complaints for at least three reasons.

First, because they work alone, they do not experience team support. Counsellors working as part of a team have chance to discuss decisions and benefit from the checks and balances that other professional colleagues can provide. They may take decisions to supervision, but there is no compulsion to do so, and anyway, by that time, it may be too late.

Second, counsellors who work as part of an organisation usually benefit from that organisation having tight procedures in place, especially a complaints procedure, and this can help defuse a situation and prevent something escalating into an official complaint to a professional counselling body. It helps the complaint to be considered and rectified (if necessary) at a local level.

Third, organisations usually have paperwork and contracts in place to help clarify for the client what counselling is, what can be expected of them, and what they can reasonably expect from the counsellor. The talking through and the signing of this paperwork helps avoid the misunderstanding and confusion that could later lead to problems and generate a complaint.

Working ethically

The recently revised ethical framework for the largest UK organisation for counselling and psychotherapy (*Ethical Framework*, BACP, July 2016), asks BACP members to commit themselves to the following:

31 We will usually provide clients with the information they ought to know in advance in order to make an informed decision about the services they want to receive and how these services will be delivered.
32 We will give careful consideration to how agreements are reached with clients and to contract with them about the terms on which our services will be provided. Attention will be given to:

a. reaching an agreement or contract that respects each client's expressed needs and choices
b. communicating terms and conditions of the agreement or contract in ways easily understood by the client and appropriate to their context
c. reaching an agreement or contract that respects each client's expressed needs and choices

d. communicating terms and conditions of the agreement or contract in ways easily understood by the client and appropriate to their context

e. stating any reasonable foreseeable limitations to a client's confidentiality or privacy

f. providing the client with a record or easy access to a record of what has been agreed

g. keeping a record of what has been agreed and of any changes or clarifications when they occur.

Of course, it could be argued that written contracts are inappropriate in certain circumstances. For example, some clients cannot read (or at least cannot read the language of the counsellor). Other clients might have special educational needs, or be children, and have difficulty in processing the mature language. Some clients may come from cultures where written contracts are regarded as a form of trickery. However, despite the exceptions, in the vast majority of cases, the above ethical commitments can, in a substantial part, be met by a good contractual process (see "Introducing a contract") that involves a written document.

In drawing up an agreement between yourself and your clients, you are wanting to communicate information that will enhance the counselling relationship, and hence increase the likelihood of the effectiveness of the counselling. You are wanting to be honest about what you want to happen and what you may choose to do if it doesn't. You are also trying to communicate to the client what they can expect from you and what you are expecting from them. A written agreement can be part of the boundary-setting procedure to provide the clear space in which the therapy can take place.

CHAPTER EIGHTEEN

If I issue a written contract, what might it include?

In broad terms, an agreement might contain information about:

- What counselling with you is likely to be like; what a client could expect.
- The appointments: How long do they last? What happens in them? How much do they cost? What happens if they are missed? How can they be paid for?
- Confidentiality; what it does and doesn't cover.
- Record-keeping and storage.
- The duration of the agreement.

I have included a full sample contract below, with my commentary. You will need to amend it according to your own preferences, needs, and understanding about what a written contract should or shouldn't contain. It is not offered as a definitive document but as a work in progress. Many counsellors will see it as far too formal and would want to modify it considerably in order to make it something they would be comfortable with. For example, you might want to shorten it and give it out to each client as a single sheet of information to discuss with them. Please see "Introducing a contract" for a discussion about raising the formal issues of the contract in the therapeutic setting.

An example contract

Counselling Agreement

Agreement between XXX and XXX

[Who is the agreement between? If you are a sole trader, you would simply need to insert your name and that of your client. If you are operating as a limited company, the agreement is between the limited company (as the limited company exists as a separate legal entity in its own right) and the client. If your business is a limited company, you might want to indicate in the document that you are the named person representing the limited company for the duration of the therapy.]

Appointments

Each session lasts for approximately XX minutes.

- It is important for effective therapy that you try to maintain regular contact.
- After every sixth session, your counsellor will review how the therapy is progressing with you.
- Your counsellor will be ready for you on time. As your counsellor does not have a waiting room, (s)he cannot accommodate you if you arrive early.
- If you arrive late for any reason, the session will finish at the appointed time.

- Your counsellor will take all reasonable precautions to ensure that the therapy space is free from interruptions. (S)he asks you to respect the therapy space too by not accepting mobile phone calls during the session.
- If you need to contact your counsellor to discuss appointment arrangements, you can reach her/him by email (email@address.co.uk) or on either of the telephone numbers (NUMBER 1, NUMBER 2). There is voicemail on both numbers and he/she will try to return your call by the end of the working day if you leave a message.

[This section attempts to address two problems that can happen around appointments (clients not realising that there is a fixed time limit and that you will end the appointment at the end of the slot if they arrive late). Most private practitioners working from home would not have waiting room space, and even if they did, would not want to encourage its use for security reasons, so its lack of availability is made clear in the agreement. The difficulty of mobile phone interruptions is anticipated and also explicitly addressed. Contact details are provided and what clients can expect in terms of return contact by the counsellor is stated. The situation in which clients could contact the counsellor out of sessions is also stated ("to discuss appointment arrangements").]

The sessions

- Counselling is a process that helps people express themselves to a professional person outside of their situation. Sometimes it can help them make choices or reach decisions about how to handle their concerns.

- Your counsellor will encourage you to talk about what is troubling you and listen to what you have to say. The aim is to help you become clearer about both the extent and the effect of the problem, and maybe to help you recognise possible solutions—ones that will work for you.
- Part of the work might involve considering what you are thinking, feeling, and doing (or not doing), and how thoughts, emotions, and behaviour all interact together.
- Part of the work might involve you finding internal resources for changes in thinking and acting, and in making the changes that you have decided on.
- In counselling, endings are important. If, for whatever reason, you make a decision to end the process, please come and discuss this with your counsellor, so that you can have a final session reviewing whatever we need to and ending the process satisfactorily.

[This section can be the most difficult to write and the one that is most likely to need adapting to your particular practice. It is an attempt to describe the counselling process and the kind of activity the client might experience during the sessions. It will obviously vary according to your particular counselling model. The above is an attempt to reflect the integrative model of the writer of this particular agreement. Some counsellors don't attempt to include this information in their agreements, but produce separate leaflets for clients about what they could expect to happen during a session. If your therapeutic model has a heavy reliance on particular techniques (asking a lot of questions, or using particular eye movements, for example), it would be important to spell that out to the client in some form (contract or leaflet) either before or at the beginning of the therapy. You would not want your clients to be surprised (and hence possibly dissatisfied).]

Fees

- The fee is £XX.00 per XX-minute session.
- Fees are normally due at the end of each session (unless otherwise agreed beforehand).
- Payment can be made by cash, cheque, credit/debit card, bank transfer, or mobile (PayM). Cheques should be made payable to XXX.

[This section spells out the important details of what the fee is for the session, when payment is due, and how payment can be made. The phrase "normally due" allows some useful flexibility should you wish to exercise it. There are three occasions when I vary that expectation. First, most EAPs or organisations expect to be invoiced at the end of the work (i.e., at the end of the six of more sessions, not at the end of every session). They usually require *at least* a month to process payments. So, when working for an EAP or an organisation, I require payment by thirty days after the invoice has been sent. Second, I sometimes vary this when working on the telephone or internet, sometimes asking clients to make a payment to confirm the initial session booking. Third, I sometimes vary this when someone other than the client has agreed to pay for the sessions. For example, a spouse or a close relative might agree to pay for the sessions and ask for an invoice for a particular number of sessions. I am happy to provide this.]

Additional work

- If it has been agreed that you can contact your counsellor on any other matter relating to your therapy between sessions and you need to speak for a prolonged length of time (longer than XX minutes), your counsellor will charge you *pro rata* for that time based on your session rate.
- Your counsellor will also bill you on a *pro rata* basis for any other reports you may ask her/him to write or read in conjunction with your therapy.

[This section spells out the terms for when any contact between sessions would be acceptable, and what the charges would be for that contact. It also makes it plain that any additional work would be charged for and at what rate.]

Health

Please do not take mood-altering drugs (unless prescribed by a GP) or alcohol before a session.

[If you are working with people who have drug or alcohol addictions, you want them to be in a capable physical and mental state so that they can participate in the counselling process when they arrive for the session with you.]

Cancellation

Your counsellor reserves the right to charge in full for missed appointments or those cancelled with less than 24 hours' notice.

[See "Should I charge for sessions where a client doesn't turn up or cancels with short notice?" Whatever you decide about charging or not charging for missed sessions, it is important to make it very clear at the beginning of the therapy.]

Confidentiality

Everything that happens in your therapy sessions remains confidential between your counsellor and you, with the following exceptions:

- Your counsellor will discuss aspects of the work with a supervisor, but your identity will remain protected.
- Your counsellor would be required to discuss the work if required to by law. (This is very rare.) For example, if you discussed acts of terrorism or serious crime or risk of serious harm to others, your counsellor would report that to the police. Similarly, if you reveal information about children or vulnerable adults being at serious risk, your counsellor would report that to the relevant authorities if you felt unable to do so yourself.
- If subpoenaed to give evidence in court, your counsellor would have to do so.
- Your counsellor may contact your GP or other medical professionals if he/she believed that you were likely to cause serious injury to yourself.

[This section seeks to explain the standard occasions when it may be necessary to breech confidentiality. Most counsellors will be familiar with these conditions, though the particular phrasing of the last one may be new to some. In private practice, there is no legal requirement to report concerns about a suicidal client to a GP (though counsellors working for different organisations must follow the requirements of the organisation concerned). However, despite the lack of a legal requirement, many private practitioners would take the view that it is part of their duty of care to the client to do so and would refuse to work with clients who were unwilling for them to disclose to their GP if suicide was seen to be a substantive risk.]

Record-keeping

- After every session (and occasionally, with your per-mission, during the session), your counsellor will make brief notes of the discussion.
- These notes do *not* constitute part of your official health record.
- Your counsellor is registered under the Data Protection Act (1998) (registration number XXX).
- Its records may be stored in a coded, encrypted, and password-protected electronic format in a cloud storage system which meets the security requirements of the DPA (98).
- Records will be kept securely for a period of XX months after counselling has ended and will then be destroyed.

[Some counsellors find it helpful to take some notes during sessions. If you work in this way, you should make that plain to the client at the beginning of the therapy.

Sometimes clients are very anxious about notes, thinking that they are part of the National Health system and that private practice counselling notes will appear on their health record. Clients who work for the NHS are often keen to check up that this isn't so. The second point above is designed to reassure these clients.

It can be helpful to let clients know if you are registered with the Information Commissioner's Office. (See "Do I need to register with the Information Commissioner's Office?".) It is important to give the client information on how the records are stored. If you do not use electronic storage, you could say that they are stored in a locked filing cabinet, for example. More and more counsellors are using their computers or the cloud to store information. If you do this, you will need to explain which security arrangements you have in place to protect the data. In the above example:

> "coded"—No names are used. Clients are given a code to protect their identity.
>
> "encrypted"—The records for the coded clients are encrypted (electronically scrambled in a way that can only be decrypted (unscrambled) using a password).
>
> "password-protected"—Access to the software used to encrypt and store the records is itself password-protected for additional security.
>
> "a cloud storage system"—Essentially on a computer accessing the internet in another location. Not stored physically on the counsellor's computer.
>
> "meets the requirements of the DPA (98)"—The 1998 Data Protection Act states that if personal data are to be sent outside of the European Economic Area, the sender needs to satisfy himself or herself that the company storing the data has rigorous security in place. If you are going to store your material using software such as Evernote, for example (based in the USA), you need to read that company's policy on data security and privacy.

If you ask thirty counsellors (including legal experts) on how long personal data has to be kept for, you are likely to get thirty different answers. A balance has to be drawn between the needs of the counsellor to keep information which could be used in defending herself or himself against a complaint, and the right of the client to have that sensitive information destroyed when it is not needed. Most counsellors would keep records for between twenty-four and seventy-two months. The BACP allows complaints to be lodged against members within three years (thirty-six months) of the ending of the professional relationship.]

Other responsibilities as a client

- You are responsible for your own thoughts, feelings, actions, and for your own personal growth.
- You are responsible for asking about anything that is unclear to you or causing you concern.
- You are responsible for communicating any changes in circumstances that might influence your therapy.

[This section is just a reminder to the client that they have responsibilities too in helping the "success" of the therapeutic relationship.]

Review

This agreement will be reviewed annually or at any other time at the request of either party.

Jurisdiction

This contract, and the work it relates to, are subject to the jurisdiction and laws of England and Wales.

[If you are working in England or Wales on the telephone or internet with clients from overseas, you should consult your professional insurance company first. Insurers are unlikely to be willing to insure you for working with clients based in America or Canada. However, some would be willing to insure you for working with clients from most other countries, but they may require you to put the above statement in your contract with clients to state quite clearly that any work is undertaken within the jurisdiction of English and Welsh law.]

I agree to the terms stated in the above agreement.
Client's signature:
Counsellor's signature:
Date:

CHAPTER NINETEEN

How could I introduce a written contract?

Of course, if you decide to use a written contract, considerable thought and care needs to go into how you might introduce it to a client. Most counsellors would not want to give a nervous client a lengthy piece of paper to read and sign at the very beginning of a first meeting. As a general principle, it is likely to be less threatening to a client if you can gently explain a few things first by talking with them, before giving them a document to read.

There is no clear right way to do this, but I introduce my contract in the following way:

- The clients arrive for the first session and I seek to put them at ease.
- I ask them if they have had counselling before and check out what their expectations are (if any) about the counselling process. I explain how I see counselling, and what their experience with me is likely to involve. I then check to see if that seems acceptable to them.

- I explain the difference between confidentiality and absolute secrecy, and explain my confidentiality policy and the rare occasions when I might need to talk to another trusted adult about what we discuss. I check out their understanding of that and acceptance of it.
- Having informally discussed two important things with them (what counselling with me is like, and what my confidentiality policy is), I then start to assess them and, if appropriate, work with them on the issues they have come to counselling for.
- Towards the end of the first session, I draw the therapeutic discussion to a close and explain that there is some administrative paperwork to complete. I ask them to fill a form in giving me their name, address, contact details, and details of their GP.
- At this point, I produce a copy of the agreement and briefly explain the purpose behind it, to help avoid any misunderstandings and help them get the most from their therapy. I ask them to take the contract home and read it and bring it with them next time. This frees them from pressure and means that they can take as long as is necessary to read the document at their own pace, and begin to formulate any questions.
- During the second session, I would spend some time informally going over the content of the contract. If necessary, I would have additional copies if they forget to bring their copy. If they had questions, I would seek to answer them. If they wanted more time to think about it, I would be happy to let them take it home again and bring it back at the next session. In nearly twenty years in private practice, I have only had two clients who refused to give me their full name, address, and GP details, and who were also

unhappy with parts of the agreement. I regretfully explained that I was unwilling to work with them, and referred them elsewhere.

If working on the telephone or internet, you would need a way of sending the contract to the client and if you require them to sign, of receiving a signed copy back, either physically through the post, or electronically.

Some counsellors would have a much shorter agreement than the long one outlined in the previous answer, and would not require a signature. However, they would probably follow a procedure similar to the one outlined above.

Some counsellors put a copy of their contract on their websites so that potential clients can read (and possibly download) it before the first meeting. Some counsellors would email clients a contract, along with other informative material, when confirming a booking.

CHAPTER TWENTY

How can I store my notes?

It is not the purpose of this answer to discuss the details of what you include in your notes, but their storage. You need to discuss with your supervisor to check that your notes are appropriate for your professional needs and comply with the requirements of the Information Commissioner's Office. However, having made your notes, how can you keep them?

To some extent, the answer to how you store them depends on the form in which you make them.

Physical notes

Physical notes are typically handwritten on paper or index cards. Historically, the advice has always been to have a code name or number or a combination of both as an identifier for each client, and to use this identifier (rather than the client's actual name) on the notes. It is recommended that the notes are then stored in a locked filing cabinet, and that the code book, enabling you to work out to whom the coded identifier refers, is also kept in a locked, but entirely separate, place. The theory is that the clients' identities can never be revealed by the code name on the notes.

If you keep physical notes, it is essential to purchase a good shredder so that physical confidential documents cannot accidentally fall into the wrong hands.

You also need to think about taking reasonable measures to protect your physical notes from accident or disaster. A locked filing cabinet might offer some protection from a leak from a temporary burst pipe, but is unlikely to offer the same protection from flooding (unless the locked filing cabinet is upstairs). If you take your notes and your code book to a different building, do you ever leave them together in a car? If you do, what would happen if your car was broken into?

Electronic notes

Although many counsellors are alarmed by the prospect of storing material electronically, it seems the norm for many more, and some would argue there are good arguments for doing so.

Computer storage

Some counsellors prefer to keep notes using their word processor or database program and store the documents on their computer. To protect client confidentiality, at least two steps can be taken:

• Protect access to the computer by ensuring that anybody logging in to the machine has to have the correct password.

- Make sure that when you have finished writing any note (using Microsoft Word or Pages, for example), you use the option available in the program to password protect that particular document (and use a different password to the one used to log in).
- Make sure that your computer has a firewall and is protected by up-to-date anti-virus software.

Arguably, if the above procedures are followed, the notes are as safe (if not safer) than any physical notes in a locked filing cabinet.

If you wanted to add a third layer of protection, you could follow the procedure recommended in physical notes and never use a client's actual identity in any note, but give the client a code identifier instead.

If you store notes on your computer, you must make sure that you back up those files on a separate back-up drive. Your computer drive will fail at some stage. And it would make sense to store that back-up drive in a separate part of the house from your computer (and preferably upstairs to help protect against the risk of flood damage).

Cloud storage

Cloud storage is where you use the services of another provider to store your notes on the internet, and not on your immediate computer. There are at least two advantages to cloud storage, and at least two possible problems to consider.

The first advantage is that your notes are always protected, whatever happens to your computer. If you suffer theft, fire, flooding, or earthquake, as long as you can get online at some point, you can retrieve your notes. The second advantage for some is the ease of accessibility. You can access your notes at home on your computer, but you could also access them (if necessary) on your smartphone or tablet. For counsellors on the move, that flexibility is important.

The first disadvantage to think through is that it goes against the Information Commissioner's principles to store client information outside the European Economic Area, and many (though not all) cloud stores are based outside the European Economic Area (especially in the United States). However, provided that the US recipient of the data is signed up to the US Department of Commerce Safe Harbor Scheme (and most reputable US companies are), the Safe Harbor scheme is recognised by the European Commission as providing adequate protection for the rights of individuals in connection with the transfer of their personal data to signatories of the scheme in the USA.

The second disadvantage is the fear that many people have about data theft and hacking on the internet. While such problems are real, many would argue that cloud storage agencies depend on security to have any business credibility and are likely to have the most secure solutions in place. They also argue that physical notes are occasionally stolen, but that doesn't stop people using locked filing cabinets. Because most cloud storage providers encrypt any material that they store, any material would probably be meaningless to a data thief.

At the time of writing, there are at least two ways of accessing cloud storage.

There are providers coming to the market place who have written specific programs for therapists, with secure storage at the forefront, that enable counsellors to write electronic notes and store them online. In the UK, existing providers include Safenotes, bacpac (and to some extent PlusGuidance). Many counsellors judge their legitimate fees to be worth the expense for the peace of mind that they offer.

Other counsellors are using more readily available non-bespoke programs such as Evernote and OneNote (both of which are effectively electronic filing cabinets). They allow you to create virtual files, and put almost anything into those files—documents, pictures, web-pages, videos, sound files, handwritten files on tablet screens—and to search them electronically. And again, available apps allow the files to be accessed by smart-phone and tablet as well as computers.

Two counsellors live together and are equal partners in a therapy business. He keeps traditional handwritten notes on index cards, with coded identities. The index cards are locked in a filing cabinet upstairs, and his code book is kept in a locked drawer in his office.

She keeps electronic notes using Evernote (a pro-gram that subscribes to the US Department of Com-merce Safe Harbor Scheme). Each client has his or her own electronic folder in Evernote, and every time a client has a session, she creates a new note of the ses-sion in that folder. Every time she creates a new note, she uses the Evernote facility to encrypt that note with a password. Occasionally, she will receive an electronic document in relation to a client (usually a PDF or a Word document). If she does, she will open the docu-ment in the appropriate program, use the program's facility to lock the document with a password, and then store the document along with her own notes in the cli-ent's file. Sometimes she will receive a physical docu-ment in relation to a client—a letter or a report. When this happens, she simply scans it in to her computer, locks the resultant PDF with a password, and stores it in the client's file.

This therapist argues that in addition to any encryption and security that the Evernote cloud itself might provide for her notes, she has provided three and sometimes four levels of security for her client's notes. In order to access her computer, her smartphone, or her tablet, anyone has to have the correct password. Then, in order to access her Evernote program, they have to have her separate Evernote password. Then, in order to access any confidential document within the program, they have to have the separate document password. Then, because all of her typed notes do not use the client's actual identity, but a coded identity, in the unlikely event that the notes were ever accessed, they would be meaningless without the separate physical code book kept in a locked drawer.

CHAPTER TWENTY-ONE

Do I need to register with the Information Commissioner's Office?

A t the time of writing, the short answer is almost certainly, "Probably yes". To get a definitive answer, you need to complete the self-assessment procedure discussed below. However, regardless of whether you are required to register by law, you might choose to register voluntarily as a way of enhancing your business image. And whether registered or not, it would be good professional and ethical practice to adhere to the principles outlined by the Commission.

The Information Commissioner's Office was set up with the aims of helping to ensure that information kept by various bodies is held responsibly so that an individual's privacy is protected. Registration with the Commission helps promote accountability, and registrants agree that their storage is guided by the principles below. Companies and individuals risk serious fines if they do not have adequate systems and security in place to protect the data they hold.

There are eight principles clearly set out by the Commission surrounding the collection and retention of data:

Fair. You must have legitimate grounds for collecting and using the personal data. You must not use the data in ways that have unjustified adverse effects on the individuals concerned.

Lawful. Be clear from the outset about why you are collecting personal data and what you intend to do with it.

Adequate. You must only hold personal data about an individual that is sufficient for the purpose you are holding it for in relation to that individual; and you must not hold more information than you need for that purpose.

Accuracy. Take reasonable steps to ensure the accuracy of any personal data you obtain; consider whether it is necessary to update the information.

Retention. The Data Protection Act does not set out any specific minimum or maximum periods for retaining personal data. Instead, it says that: Personal data processed for any purpose or purposes shall not be kept for longer than is necessary for that purpose or those purposes.

Rights. Personal data has to be processed respecting the rights of the individual. There are several of these rights, but the most commonly understood is a right of access to a copy of the information comprised in an individual's personal data.

Security. Appropriate organisational and technical measures need to be taken to prevent unlawful processing or loss of the data.

International. Personal data should not be transferred to a country or territory outside the European Economic Area unless that country or territory ensures an adequate level of protection for the rights and freedoms of data subjects in relation to the processing of personal data.

The self-assessment

Under the Data Protection Act, individuals and organisations that process personal information need to register with the Information Commissioner's Office (ICO), unless they are exempt.

The Information Commissioner's Office provides a five-minute self-assessment test to enable you to see if you need to register: https://ico.org.uk/for-organisations/register/self-assessment/

- Are you a not-for-profit organisation that qualifies for an exemption?

  All private practitioners would have to answer "No" to this. We are self-employed in business to make a living (or profit).
- Does your business or organisation process information only for judicial functions?

  Again, the answer for most of us is "No".
- Are you processing personal information?

  As "processing" information includes "obtaining, recording, storing" it, the answer is clearly "Yes".
- Do you process the information electronically?

  If you use emails or texts to correspond with clients, or hold information about them on any electronic device (including smart phones or tablets), the answer is "Yes".
- Is your organisation responsible for deciding how the information is processed?

  Unless you subcontract out to another organisation for dealing with all the information (correspondence, accounts, for example), the answer is "Yes".
- Do you process personal information only for personal, family, household, or recreational reasons?

  You are running a business, so the answer is "No".

- Are you only processing information to maintain a public register?

  "No".

- Do you process personal data only for staff adminis-tration, advertising, marketing or public relations, or accounts or records?

  I take the answer to this to be "No". I am collecting and using information primarily about members of the public who become my clients. They are not my staff.

- Do you process individuals' information only for staff administration?

  "No". I am collecting and using information prima-rily about members of the public who become my clients. They are not my staff.

- Do you process individuals' information for advertis-ing, marketing, or public relations?

  The answer for me is "No".

If your answers agree with mine, you need to register.

The misconceptions

Hand-written material

There is a common belief amongst counsellors that because they may keep hand-written notes, they do not need to register. There is some truth in this belief. Registration is required only when information pro-cessing is carried out electronically. If all information, including correspondence to clients, referrals, and cli-ent notes, are processed manually, then there is no requirement to register. However, hand-written mate-rial may be covered by the legislation in the future, and most counsellors who think they don't process information electronically are increasingly likely to do so. Emails, texts, smart phones, computers, and tablets are becoming routine in business communication.

The European Economic Area

Many counsellors assume that they comply with the Commission's eight principles because they genuinely believe that they do not send data outside the European Economic Area. However, they are almost certainly being naïve in that belief.

Most, if not all, of them are sending it outside the EEA without realising it. People using electronic calendars and directories provided by most of the free email providers, or using the cloud to store and back up information (an increasingly common—and some would argue "sensible"—practice), are almost certainly sending client data to the United States of America, where a lot of these companies have their storage servers.

Fortunately, transfer of data is permitted if the country or territory in question ensures an adequate level of protection for the rights and freedoms of data subjects in relation to the processing of personal information. In the United States, many of the large companies that are recipients of the data are signed up to the US Department of Commerce Safe Harbor Scheme. The Safe Harbor Scheme is recognised by the European Commission as providing adequate protection for the rights of individuals in connection with the transfer of their personal data to signatories of the scheme in the USA.

If you use any software solutions in your business to help you in any way, check out the small print of the companies' data-protection policies.

CHAPTER TWENTY-TWO

What about working for agencies?

When I first started in private practice, my then supervisor told me that the majority of her work came from employee assistance providers (EAPs) and other agencies. At the time, I found it hard to imagine that I would ever get work from an agency. I currently receive regular work from four EAPs and over the years have worked for four others at different stages. Approximately fifty per cent of my income now comes from such sources. For private practitioners looking to regularly work with a significant number of clients, they are a good source of referrals.

Broadly speaking, there are three types of external referral sources providing two types of loosely distinctive (but also overlapping) types of work.

Employee assistance providers

EAPs are companies that offer to deal with the limited counselling needs of the workforce employed by other organisations and companies. For an employer, it makes good sense to provide a level of care for your employees. One estimate is that mental health issues are costing British businesses £70 billion per year— 4.5 per cent of GDP (http://www2.cipd.co.uk/pm/peoplemanagement/b/weblog/archive/2014/04/01/employers-launch-campaign-to-slash-163-70-billion-cost-of-mental-illness.aspx). Whether or not this claim is true, counselling can certainly help employees tackle stress, help with life and work demands that affect performance, and reduce absenteeism.

Company employees are usually given a telephone number for the EAP that their employer has a contract with so that they can contact the EAP directly. Sometimes the company HR department will advise an employee to contact the EAP. The EAP will usually do a brief telephone assessment and offer the client a limited number of counselling sessions—and depending on the nature of the contract, this counselling will be offered by telephone, email, or face to face. Once the client details have been obtained, a counsellor who works for the EAP as an associate, and who is geographically nearest the client (or who has expressed a willingness to work by telephone or email), will be asked if she or he wishes to take the referral.

Clients from EAPs usually present with the following kinds of issues:

- work-related issues, such as: bullying, stress and workload, traumatic workplace incidents, performance issues, interpersonal difficulties, facing dismissal or redundancy;
- personal issues, such as: bereavement, ill-health, divorce, problems with relatives or children, miscarriage, depression, anxiety;
- a combination of the above.

Rehabilitation agencies and solicitors

Another group of companies work with employers, or more usually insurance companies, and are concerned with helping individuals following some kind of traumatic incident that has seriously affected their physical or mental health. Typical examples would be people who have suffered a physical assault at work, or who have been involved in road traffic accidents. An insurance company is usually the agency footing the bill for the work, and by the time clients are referred to you they will usually have been referred to a doctor (and possibly a psychologist) who will have dealt with any medical issues and who will almost certainly have recommended a period of counselling to deal with any ongoing mental health problems.

Sometimes the insurance company will employ a rehabilitation agency to co-ordinate the various parties, and they will contact you and make the referral. Sometimes a solicitor acting on behalf of the insurance company will contact you directly.

Other companies

Some employers (typically smaller, local ones) decide to cut out the middle person (an EAP) and contact a counsellor directly. If they receive good feedback about your service from the employee (or employees) they refer to you, you may well be able to build up a good long-term relationship with their HR department. Over the years, I have received a number of referrals from a local school (teaching staff), a waste company, a bus company, and a housing association.

Number of sessions (short-term work)

With EAPs, the maximum number of sessions can vary with the client and with each provider. However, the usual number is six. It is usually possible to ask for an extension of a few sessions once the counselling has started, and one or two extra sessions may be granted in justified cases. Although the usual number is six, I was once offered two sessions, as well as being offered three and four sessions, and five is now the norm with one particular EAP.

With rehabilitation agencies and solicitors, I have usually found there to be more flexibility (more financial resources available). I have found there to be more willingness to extend the period of counselling, provided you can justify doing so. Initial contracts may be for six sessions, but I have often worked for between twelve and twenty sessions with such clients.

With individual companies, I have found that they are often aware of the EAP six-session norm. However, depending on the company and the nature of the client's presenting issue, there is sometimes more flexibility than what you might typically expect from an EAP.

Please note that all work that is funded in the ways described above by somebody other than the individual client is short-term work. As a counsellor, you need to be happy with this concept from a philosophical point of view, and be sufficiently skilled to deal with it in the sessions (few counsellors are trained in short-term work). If you have a view that deplores such a concept and a theoretical model that would make it impossible for you to conduct a six-session intervention, you need to refuse any requests to do such work. Most EAPs require their affiliates to explain the limited scope of the counselling in the first session and to set agreed, realistic targets for the work.

The messy but important details

I once watched a documentary about how the London Underground functioned before it was a united company and comprised lots of different individual companies with partial routes and separate ticketing procedures. To make what is now a relatively simple journey across the capital could involve travelling on trains run by different companies, each charging a separate fare and requiring different tickets. It was a complicated experience.

I often think of that documentary when working with an EAP client. Each company has a different set of requirements and different forms. These differences mean that before an EAP client comes to the session, I have to remind myself of the procedures for that company and complete the requirements both at the beginning and end of each session. Such differences are:

- Having the client assessed by the company, or by them requiring you to do it at the first meeting.
- Knowing what, if any, documents clients are required to sign at the beginning of the work, and whether or not those documents have to be kept or forwarded to the EAP.
- Whether or not the EAP requires you to collect any psychometric data (for example, CORE10, GAD7, or PHQ9), and if so, whether it is required from each session, or at various points during the intervention, or just at the beginning and ending.
- Whether or not you are required to submit notes, and if so, whether they are required from each session,

or at various points during the intervention, or just at the beginning and ending.

- If you are required to submit notes, whether or not they are to be emailed, entered into a particular form on paper and emailed, or submitted via an internet portal.
- What the procedures are for a DNA or late cancellation, and whether or not you get paid for such events.
- Whether you are required to submit your own invoice or complete one of their physical forms, or submit your invoice via an internet portal.

The other important detail concerns payment. Most EAPs and agencies require you to submit an invoice once the work is completed. They then usually promise to pay from between thirty to sixty days after the receipt of the invoice. If you start work in January, it is unlikely to be finished until mid-February, and you are unlikely to be paid until mid-March at the earliest.

You can see the extra complications that such work imposes on a counsellor, especially if they end up working for more than one EAP. The good thing about being in private practice is that you can always refuse any future work if you find that things don't work out in the way that you want them to. Over the years, I have stopped working for two EAPs and one rehabilitation agency because of what I judged to be the administrative incompetence of one, and because of the real difficulty of getting payment out of the others.

How can I get such work?

The EAP Association has a list of their members (http://www.eapa.org.uk/find-an-eap-provider/), and you could contact the EAPs directly. If they are looking to employ affiliates in your area, you may be lucky and get some referrals. However, all my work for EAPs and rehabilitation agencies and companies has come from them contacting me. I think if you want such work, it is essential to have a strong web presence by having your own website and from being listed in directories such as the BACP one. If an agency wants a counsellor in your area, and you have a strong web presence, then it won't be too hard for them to find your details and to contact you.

And, of course, if you have had any professional training in a model that lends itself to short-term work, that can only help.

CHAPTER TWENTY-THREE

Can I work with clients in their own homes?

I had a relative who initially trained as a hairdresser. When she first started work, all of her hairdressing was done in a salon in the city centre. After she had interrupted her career to have children, she found it easier to get back to work by operating from home. She converted a downstairs office in her house into a mini-salon and started to build up a base of loyal customers who regularly came to her address. As she and her customers grew older, she started to receive more requests for her to visit her "regulars" in their own homes. Once it became known that she was willing to do this, her customer base increased considerably as she not only got new individuals who enjoyed the luxury of being visited rather than making the journey to her, but she also got several good contracts from various local nursing homes who wanted a mobile hairdresser to work with their residents.

Is it OK for counsellors to travel to clients and work with them in their own homes?

On the surface, there are some similarities between counsellors and hairdressers, and there are certain attractions to visiting clients in their homes. Both counsellors and hairdressers are aiming to provide a service to meet the specific needs of their clients, and the delivery of this service is not dependent on any particular location (provided certain basics are in place).

And travelling to clients rather than having them come to you does have some advantages. For example, if you travelled to all of your clients, you would not have the expenses and inconveniences of having to work from a fixed location. There would be no rent or other location expenses to pay (for example, heating, lighting). Compared to working from home, there would be fewer worries about having to book appointments around family arrangements, or about tidying and cleaning rooms and hallways to make them "client acceptable". Compared to working from rented rooms, there would be less likelihood of having to wait around in a location that you had paid for when no client turned up. However, even if you did allow yourself to visit clients, it is unlikely that your entire professional practice would be conducted away from your base. Even the travelling hairdresser mentioned above continued to see several clients at her home.

As far as I am aware, there is no law forbidding counsellors to travel to their clients, and as private practitioners, you are able to make your own decisions about where, when, and how you work. However, when thinking about travelling to clients, you need to consider the following factors: insurance, costs, safety, conditions, access, and alternatives.

Insurance

There probably won't be a problem, but you need to check with your professional insurer that you are covered for visiting clients and working in their homes. If you are using your car to travel to them, you will need to make sure that your car insurance covers you for business use rather than for ordinary domestic usage. Also, if your premium is related to the amount of annual mileage you do, make sure that you allow for any extra mileage that your travel is likely to generate. The extra car insurance costs could be factored into the fee you charge, in addition to the issues discussed immediately below.

Costs

Don't be naive about the real costs involved. In addition to the fee that you would normally charge for your professional services, there are two other significant things to charge for.

Perhaps the most obvious one is mileage. At the time of writing, you can claim £0.45 per mile as a legitimate business expense against tax for the first 10,000 miles of business travel, and £0.25 per mile after that. (You can check current rates at https://www.gov.uk/government/publications/rates-and-allowances-travel-mileage-and-fuel-allowances/travel-mileage-and-fuel-rates-and-allowances.) If £0.45 per mile seems a lot, it isn't once you consider what it actually costs per mile to run your car. In addition to fuel, there is insurance, servicing, repairs, tyres, road tax, and depreciation in value of your vehicle. There are now apps available for smartphones to help you calculate the actual cost per mile of running your car, and if you do the sums, the answer would come far closer to £0.45 than you think. If you are travelling to a client, it would be wise to charge them £0.45 for each mile there and back to cover your travel costs.

The second cost factor is travelling time. Say it takes up to 30 minutes to travel to a client and 30 minutes to return, how much would you charge for your travelling time? You could decide not to charge for travelling time. If you do this, then you are making a decision to reduce your professional fee. If a visit actually takes two hours—one for the session, and one for the travelling—and if you normally charge £40 per session, by not charging for travelling time, you have effectively reduced your rate to £20 a session. That would be very difficult to sustain if you wanted to earn a living.

You could decide not to bother with specific amounts for travelling time, but simply increase your session rates for clients you have to travel to. The problem with this is that it is unfair because clients close to you end up paying far more and clients far away get a cheap deal.

If you decide to charge for travelling time, you are left with the dilemma of how much to charge. I have seen one invoice from a particular practitioner who charged £40 per session and £80 per hour (pro rata for any part thereof), though I was never able to ask how he justified the expense. Some practitioners argue that if they are travelling, they are away from base and not able to earn what they would be if there were at base, so they charge the same rate for travelling as they do for counselling. Some counsellors feel uncomfortable with that, and charge a proportion of their session fee for travelling time.

Suppose I was asked to work with a client approximately 12 miles from my home. If I agreed to that, before the first session I would want to give them a quotation in writing of the cost of each session.

Counselling fee for 50-minute session	£40.00
Mileage (2 × 12) @£0.45 per mile	£10.80
Travel time (2 × 30 minutes) @£25 per hour	£25.00
	£75.80

If you do not have a lot of clients, being willing to travel might be one way of increasing your client load. However, busy therapists are unlikely to be willing to travel a lot as it becomes uneconomic. If they are charging only £25 per hour to travel, they can earn more per hour by staying at their base, especially if they have a backlog of clients waiting to see them.

Safety

It could be quite dangerous going into a stranger's home for the first time. If they come to you, at least you know your own environment and can arrange it appropriately. However, if visiting a new client, you are literally on unknown territory. Before agreeing to work with an unknown person in an unknown environment, it is essential to do at least two things: first, do an informal risk assessment; second, have a buddy system and plan in place (see "What could I do to increase my personal safety when working alone?").

To do an informal risk assessment, you need to have contact, and I would suggest that you do this over the telephone or via teleconference. What are your instincts telling you about the safety of working with this person? Is there anything obvious for you to worry about? Do they seem happy to comply with the conditions that you are stipulating (see Conditions below)? Of course, such informal assessments and listening to your subjective impressions cannot guarantee your safety, but they might stop you going into an obviously dangerous situation.

It is absolutely imperative that you have a buddy system in place—an agreement with a trusted colleague or family member that you will phone them soon after entering the premises, and just before leaving, to confirm that everything is OK. If you do not phone, they will have an agreed plan of action to put into operation. The first action might just be to phone you to see if you have forgotten to phone them. The second action might be more serious and involve contacting the police.

Remember too that, although you have given some control about the meeting to the client, you can keep control of the timing. You don't have to agree to visiting after dark if you don't want to.

Conditions

If a client travels to you, you have more control over the environment. You can turn off telephones, televisions, and radios to avoid the possibility of interrupting distractions. You can be more confident about making sure that any other people in the building are well away from your session. You can control the decor and arrangement of the therapeutic space.

If you are visiting clients, you will need to establish some "ground rules" about what you expect to happen if counselling is to take place. For example, these "ground rules" might include the following:

- an understanding that no other adults, children, or pets be present in the room during therapy (unless you have previously agreed beforehand to allow this under particular exceptional circumstances);

- that all potentially distracting equipment (televisions, radios, computers, sound systems) in the space, or within earshot of the room, be turned off;
- that the client cannot undertake any other activity (for example, child-minding, ironing, washing up, knitting) during the session;
- that the sessions are not casual social occasions and will start and finish on time.

On most occasions, the above rules are unlikely to be necessary. However, the author knows of one therapist who refused to conduct a session with a client who wanted to talk to him while standing at the sink and doing washing up. He also knows of a therapist who often had to insist that the client's carer and children left the room at the start of the session and that the television was turned off.

Access

On the positive side, being willing to travel to clients occasionally does mean that some clients would no longer be denied counselling because of illness or circumstances. If clients have a physical or a psychological condition that prevents them from travelling, or if they do not drive and cannot easily access alternative transport, a visiting counsellor could be one way that they can access therapy.

In nearly twenty years of private practice, I have worked with only three clients in their own environment. One was an extremely ill man who was too unwell to travel; two were a very elderly couple who were unable to make a long and difficult journey on public transport.

Alternatives

Today, there are several alternatives to travelling to a client's home to conduct therapy (see "How can I increase access to my services?"). The telephone and videoconference mean that communication across distance and without travel is relatively easy and cheap. And while such methods are not the same as face-to-face counselling, or problem free, most clients are able and willing to access and use the technology, especially when the session fee, plus fuel charges, plus travelling time charges for visiting them, are spelled out to them.

Visiting clients at home is still (and will always be) an option in some circumstances, but I suspect that requests for it may become fewer.

CHAPTER TWENTY-FOUR

Will I have to work evenings and weekends?

The short answer is "No". You are free to work whenever you want to. However, part of running a successful business involves delivering products or services that people want, at a price they can afford, in the quantity they need, at a time when they want it.

One of the local counselling charities I know operates on weekdays between 9:00 a.m. and 3:00 p.m. I am aware of their reasons for this. Limited and precarious funding means that they cannot employ enough staff to deliver the service they want to. Operating on a Saturday would mean closing one day during the week. And they don't have the extra staff to provide the cover to make the centre safe in the evenings. As a result of these restrictions, the client base they are able to serve is inevitably restricted.

The clients who attend the centre are mainly those who are not working outside the home, either by choice or because of unemployment. Very occasionally, a client who is self-employed, or someone who is able to manage their own work commitments, will attend, but this is relatively rare. People in paid work are either unable to regularly get time off to attend counselling, or are unwilling to ask for it because of the stigma still attached to counselling by some, so by operating the hours that it does, this counselling charity is unable to serve a large proportion of the general population.

Of course, there are good reasons for deciding not to work in the evenings or at weekends.

For some counsellors, it is part of their choice to maintain a healthy work/life balance. They are choosing to draw boundaries around their work in this particular way.

For some counsellors, it could be about safety. (See "What could I do to increase my personal safety?") If you feel physically isolated or personally vulnerable, it may be a wise decision to not see clients when there are likely to be fewer people or less light about.

For some counsellors, there could be real practical difficulties about evening or weekend work. If you hire premises, it may be that they are not available at those times. If you work from home, there can be considerable difficulties factoring the likely movements of other household members into arranging appropriate evening appointments. Partners may be willing to be regularly banished from the house or consigned to the bedroom or kitchen for an hour or two, but teenage children are less likely to be sympathetic or compliant.

On the other hand, if you are able to offer some evening or weekend appointments, you are making it more likely that you will attract clients. Private practice depends on clients paying for your professional services, and the people most likely to have money to pay you are people who are in work, and these are the people who will want evening or weekend appointments. If you decide at some stage to increase your expertise and range of services and offer couple counselling, you are only ever likely to get couple bookings in the evenings or at weekends. The difficulties of two people getting time off work to attend are too great.

If you do decide to operate in less sociable hours, that doesn't mean that your work/life balance has to be unboundaried. Most counsellors who offer appointments in these less sociable slots compensate by taking mornings or afternoons off at other times during the week. Some counsellors will work Saturday mornings, but I know of very few who work outside of that slot at the weekend. When starting out, there is a danger that you are so keen to get work that you might say "Yes" to any request. It is important to have made a strong decision about when you will and won't work and to keep to that.

My experience is that for clients who want a particular time for counselling, the most frequently requested slots are:

- 1:30 p.m. so that parents can go on to school afterwards to pick up their children;
- 4:00 p.m. so that people can leave work a bit early and pop in for counselling on their way home;
- 5:30 p.m. so that people can finish work on time and pop in for counselling on their way home;
- 8:00 p.m. so that people have time to get home and have a meal before "turning out" again;
- Saturday mornings, so that people who work away in the week have had chance to return home on Friday night.

I have now chosen never to have appointments between 5:00 p.m. and 7:00 p.m. on weekdays, or on Friday evenings or weekends. Despite several requests for appointments in those times, I can now happily say that I have learned that it is OK to say "No".

CHAPTER TWENTY-FIVE

What should I do if I bump into my clients in my locality?

The chances are that, unless you are working on the internet or telephone with clients who are overseas or who live in a different part of the country, the majority of your clients will be local, and there is a high probability that you will "bump" into them at least once at some stage in the future.

I have heard of a counsellor who went for a coffee in a well-known chain shop only to end up (by genuine chance) sitting close to a lady (one of his current clients) and her husband (who didn't know that she was going for counselling and who didn't know that she was having an affair with his best friend). I also know a counsellor who was invited to a large birthday party at a hotel. When he arrived and looked at the formal place settings at the tables where the food was being served, he noticed, to his horror, that he was sitting at the same table as one of his current male clients and the client's mother (who didn't know that her son had been for quite a long period of counselling). What would you have done in these situations?

I suspect that some counsellors would have a very strict rule about chance meetings with present and former clients outside the counselling room, and would do as much as possible to ignore the clients, and treat them as strangers. Such a rule may reinforce the notion that the relationship is professional and should not exist outside of the counselling room. However, to my mind, it seems a brutal way of maintaining a point. It also feels very strange to me to have to completely ignore someone who may have spent some considerable time working with you, and with whom you may have shared some appropriately professional deep communication.

Equally, it would also be inappropriate to engage in lengthy conversation about any matter (be it therapeutic or general). Some clients do actually want to be our friends and maintain contact with us, and we should be careful not to do anything to encourage that. I may occasionally "bump" into my GP, my dentist, or my solicitor in the street, but I know that I have a professional relationship with them and that, although they may smile and say hello in passing, they do not want to stop and chat for hours about my stiff joints, my false teeth, or my mother's will.

The solution I have found works best for me (and I fully accept that others—particularly those who are strong on rigid boundaries—may disagree with me) involves two stages: explaining the notion of a professional relationship, and empowering the client.

A professional relationship

Because you can never predict when you might meet a client outside of the therapy sessions, I try to raise the issue of possible contact early on in the relationship. Having thought about and discussed a possible encounter, we are more likely to be able to handle it in a way that avoids misunderstandings and problems. I explain that even though they may tell me some very private and emotional things, and although I will listen intently and work hard to help them help themselves, I have a professional relationship with them and can never be their friend (even if they wanted that). I explain that there have to be boundaries in place for good reasons. My written contract discourages contact, other than administrative necessities, between and after sessions. Any chance meeting would have to limit any contact.

Empower the client

Having established the need for boundaries, I then give the control for any chance meeting back to the clients. I explain that I fully understand that there may be situations where the clients do not want to be seen to know me (as in the two awkward examples given above) and that I would not acknowledge them and fully understand if they completely ignored me. Similarly, if they felt comfortable and wanted to say hello and briefly pass the time of day, I would be very happy to do that. However, I would wait for them to make the first move. So, in my relatively small town, I sometimes see a client who smiles and says hello in passing, and then am completely ignored by the same client when he is in the company of certain others. And that's OK for both of us.

The awkward two

What would you have done in the two situations described above? In theory, it may have been possible for the counsellor to have found a different seat in the cafe, and to have asked for a different table at the hotel. However, such changes risk drawing attention to the awkward situations and could have made them worse. Clearly in both situations, the counsellor indicating that he knew that client would have risked betraying part of the client's confidentiality (that the client was attending counselling). Fortunately, the counsellors and clients, in both situations, completely ignored each other. There was plenty to discuss at the next therapy sessions.

CHAPTER TWENTY-SIX

How can I increase the chances of an enquiry becoming a client?*

Helping secure a first appointment

Because I want to work with clients rather than look at a list of enquiries that never made it to my front door, I want to do everything humanly possible to help them make that first assessment appointment happen (if appropriate). Of course, if I worked as part of a larger counselling service, I may have the luxury of systems and support and of other people helping make that appointment happen—perhaps a trained receptionist to listen to the client's first tentative steps, answer questions, and book an appointment. In the early days of my practice, when I frequently couldn't pick up the landline (because of being with a client, or because of being away from the office), all I could offer my timid enquirers was an answerphone that many of

---

*A version of the material in this answer originally appeared in Rye, J. (2013). Closing the gap. *Private Practice*, Spring: 22–25. Used with BACP's kind permission.

them failed to respond to. I "lost" a lot of clients, and potentially a lot of business.

Review the telephone contact options

First impressions are important, and it is essential for any therapist working from home to be able to know when the landline rings whether it is a personal or a business call. For some people, the best way to do this is to bear the expense of two landlines. However, at least one phone service provider (BT) has a service called Call Sign which, for small monthly fee, enables the therapist to have two separate numbers on a single landline. Because each of the numbers has a separate ringtone, whoever answers the phone is able to tell whether the incoming call is a personal or business one.

In an age when mobile usage has become routine and when text messaging is one of the most common means of communication, it is important to offer potential clients the option of mobile contact. In my experience, some new enquirers wanting to speak will elect to phone my business landline number. However, I am receiving an increasing number of new enquiries via text or voice message to my mobile. Texting enables the potential client to have direct access to me but without the potential embarrassment of having to speak (rather like an email enquiry), and, at the same time, in some ways feels less impersonal than leaving a voicemail message. It is relatively easy to book a first appointment in this way—though if the texting becomes developed, I will always seek permission to phone back to discuss further. Whatever you think about texting, the reality is that it removes some of the stress of initial contact for some clients.

One of the best things to improve the quality of my business telephone contact with potential clients has been the discovery of a virtual office assistant service. There are a number of companies offering to answer calls in your business name, to take any messages, and then to email them to you. If you keep an online calendar (Google Calendar, for example), keeping your bookings private but showing when you have free slots, some virtual assistants will also book appointments for you.

There is usually a set-up fee, and then you are given a landline number to divert your phone to, and a fee is charged for each call answered. When my clients arrive, I simply divert all my calls to my virtual assistant. Calls are answered in my business name and any messages (usually a name and number to call back) are immediately emailed to me. Obviously, the assistants will not be able to (or try to) answer professional questions, but just say that the enquirer needs to speak to me and that I will phone back at the first available opportunity. When I am free to answer calls again, I simply call the enquirer.

Prices for such services vary, as does the quality of answering. Shop around and test them out. The one I use, NoMissedCalls (http://www.nomissedcalls.co.uk), has modest set-up and answering charges. Because there are significant times during the working week when I am out of the office or have to turn off the ringers on my phones, a virtual office assistant means that my calls can be taken by another human being rather than a recording device, and this, in my experience, increases the chance of therapy taking place. For me, it is a relatively cheap way of buying a professional service that gives me peace of mind and helps me gain, rather than lose, clients.

Possible booking solutions

We all know that actually speaking to potential clients is really useful. It enables us to answer questions and to negotiate the potential logistical problems of matching our diary with theirs. Before the internet and mobile phones (yes, some of us can actually remember those dark times), enquirers had to pick up a phone and speak.

However, the reality is that more and more clients are no longer doing that in the first instance—either because of shyness, or simply just because they feel more at home with email and text, and automatically default to those methods. Most of the email enquiries I get can be summarised as follows: "I have a problem with X. Do you think you can help me?" Historically, this would then have started an email exchange of many letters. Me: "Yes, we can work together. When would you like an appointment?" Client: "I can do Mondays, but not this week" etc., etc. Although it did eventually lead to some appointments, I found there were several problems with it. It tended to take time, and it was frustrating trying to get agreement on specifics when the answers to each part of the equation sometimes took days to arrive (by which time availability had often changed anyway). And because it was time-consuming, some clients disappeared. One colleague has told me that he is sure that some of the email enquiries he gets are ones that are sent to many potential therapists (possibly email addresses taken from the BACP website, or the Counselling Directory, for example). There is an element of, "If you want my business, you had better respond quickly".

I have now found two ways of trying to cut down the lengthy, vague email exchanges and of making it much easier for clients to book a specific time-slot quickly. The first thing I have done is put an appointment request form on my websites (see, for example, http://www.kingslynncounselling.co.uk/contact-your-kings-lynn-counsellor.html). This form isn't a vague contact form, but asks clients questions about which days and times they are likely to be available for an appointment. If they complete it and submit it to me, it enables me to immediately see when they are likely to be free. I then select a slot and offer them an appointment.

I used to be afraid of website forms. I knew enough about website construction to be acutely aware that you needed to have read more than "An Idiot's Guide to Website Coding" in order to be able to construct forms that actually worked. However, these days there are plenty of services offering simple ways of constructing forms and then giving you the code to insert into your website. In my view, one of the best is the free form application that is part of the Google Drive service. You simply sign up for a free Google account, go to the "drive" option, select "create", and then choose "form". If you can use a word processor or desktop publishing software, then you will be able to create a form with ease. There are four things about this service that I find compellingly useful:

- The forms are easy to create and modify.
- You have the option of storing information. The information from all form submissions can be automatically put into a spreadsheet so that you can access it easily.
- You have *immediate* feedback. (This can be important—see "Speed and redundancy" below.) Each time your form is submitted, you receive an email informing you. The information isn't left hanging around for days. You can respond at your first opportunity.

- Even if you don't have a website, you can still use the service. You can cut and paste either a URL for your form, or the complete form itself, into an email to send the enquirer.

If the potential clients don't fill in the form but send an email, a second way of managing the enquiries is not to ask them when *they* are available, but to reveal which slots *you* have available. Until recently, I did this by typing a range of free slots into my reply email. Then I discovered free online scheduling services. These services require you to keep your appointments in an electronic calendar such as the one in Outlook, or in Google (something I do anyway so that I can sync my appointments across my desktop, laptop, phone, and tablet and access it anywhere at any time). They then link with your calendar, not to reveal your appointments, but to see which slots you have free. You simply send your clients the link to the scheduler which shows your availability. The client then selects the slot she or he wants, and the scheduler emails you and automatically updates your diary.

Services such as Touchbase (http://www.touchbase. it/), ScheduleOnce (http://www.scheduleonce.com), and Vcita (http://www.vcita.com/) offer online scheduling. You can also make your available slots visible online using the free to join secure counselling portal PlusGuidance (http://www.plusguidance.com). Some of the free calendar apps, such as Outlook, offer the ability to send available slots to your clients so that they can easily select one.

Speed and redundancy

The systems I have in place enable me to respond professionally and quickly to any enquiry. And as counsellors, we are aware that non-verbal messages are very powerful. I want the efficiency of my non-verbal communication, and its speed, and its quality to say to the client, "Your enquiry really is important to me, and I really am interested in us having a meeting to see if it would be appropriate for us to work together."

There are two more things that I try to do to reinforce the above message. First, I always try to respond quickly. At the first available opportunity I will call back or respond to the form, the email, or the text. Not only do I not want to lose the client to another therapist (and he or she may be contacting several), but I want the client to know that I am serious about the possibility of working with them. Wherever possible, I usually try to reply immediately, and the response I often get is: "Thanks for getting back to me so quickly. I appreciate that."

Second, in order to reinforce the above message, I try, if possible, to communicate about that first appointment in more than one way. In my view, it helps add a concrete reality to the future appointment, and in some cases increases the speed of the message (a text might be read immediately whereas an email might not be read for hours). If a client phones to book an appointment and leaves a mobile number as a contact point, I will text a confirmation of the details that we have spoken about. If a client emails or submits the form, in addition to replying via email, I will also text a summary of the details arranged so the client gets an immediate response.

Listening to need

Whichever technical solutions you decide to employ to take enquiries, it is, of course, imperative to use your skills to listen to what clients are saying, help them identify what they want, and, if possible, assure them that you are likely to be able to help them help themselves in some way. Sometimes it may be necessary to simply offer them an exploratory session to enable you both to talk at greater length.

The people contacting you will be nervous, especially if using the phone. On occasions, they may have a rambling story to tell, or be confused in what they are asking. You are likely to increase their chances of becoming clients if you can:

- summarise the need: "I can hear that you are in a lot of pain right now in that relationship, and you feel that you are not being heard."
- offer hope of the need being addressed: "I can't promise miracles, but I do have several years' experience of helping clients find a way of expressing themselves in difficult relationships, and of understanding a bit more about how they might have got into that situation."
- offer an action path: "I sense you called me to make enquiries because you were wanting to do something. Looking in my diary, I see that I have some possible free appointment slots in the next two weeks. Would you like to book one now, or would you like to think some more?"

Miscellany

CHAPTER TWENTY-SEVEN

How can I get a website?

Of course, there are many counsellors who have run successful businesses without ever having had a website. However, these days, more so than ever, it makes sense to advertise on the internet because that is where most clients would go to look for a counsellor.

Website designers

There are plenty of people out there willing to design a website for you, and the increase in supply of available talent has brought some of the prices down. If you decide to go down this route, you might like to consider the following:

- Ask to see what other work they have done to assess their style and talent before making a commitment.
- Make sure you understand how easy it would be to make changes to the site (such as increasing or lowering your session prices) and how much such changes would cost.

- Ask whether a dedicated URL (website address) and email account is included in the package.
- Ask whether they are publishing and hosting your site, or simply designing it.
- Ask whether the website will be search-engine optimised and mobile-friendly and tablet-friendly (see "Search engine optimisation", below).

Although I have met many counsellors who now have impressive sites having gone down this route, I have also come across people who have had bad experiences. Three common mistakes are:

- Going for the cheapest, when the cheapest isn't necessarily the best. Using a keen teenager who is the relative of a friend of a friend might result in a cheap website. However, you might then have to pay someone else to turn it into a website that you wouldn't be embarrassed to be associated with.
- Not writing down and discussing clearly with the designer beforehand precisely what you want. Once the designer has spent hours creating your site, they won't take too kindly to suddenly being presented with requests ("Can we include this video?" "I want people to be able to fill a form in?") that weren't included in the original brief. Spend plenty of time thinking about what you precisely want beforehand. You wouldn't expect a builder to build a house for you and then be asked to change the size of the rooms once it was complete.
- Not having search engine optimisation. If your site doesn't come high in the search engine rankings, it will be invisible to potential clients.

There are now a few organisations that specialise in creating websites for individuals and organisations, and some produce therapy sites. They try to take the pain out of the whole business of getting a URL, a website, a dedicated email, and hosting. It is worth shopping around to see what each offers. See, for example, Citizen Click (http://citizenclick.co.uk/), You Can Consulting (http://www.youcanconsulting.co.uk/), Health Hosts (http://www.healthhosts.com/).

Online website builders

For individuals who are reasonably IT literate, there are now a number of sites that make the self-creation of websites moderately easy. These sites offer the subscriber a choice of template into which the users type their own material. If you are competent enough to use a word processor or create a PowerPoint display, then you almost certainly have enough IT skills to learn how to interact with one of these template sites. Because their most basic features are usually available for free (though you would obviously pay for more advanced features), you have nothing to lose by trying them out and seeing if you can get one to work for you.

There are several advantages to using such packages:

- Within the options available, you retain control of the design. If you don't like the look of your website, you can usually change the design by selecting another template and simply clicking a button.
- You have complete control of the content. If you want to change your therapy prices, you can change the details whenever you want. If you want to add a page about another specialism you offer, you can easily do it.
- You easily publish your site on the internet at the press of a button.

- Many of the packages include the option to add video or pictures or audio files, should you wish to do so.
- Most packages include the option to have a response form so that potential clients can fill in details and contact you if you wish them to do so.
- Some packages have a "shop" option that you can link to a PayPal account. So, for example, you could use this to sell any support material you have written, or get clients to pay for sessions, or take bookings for training events.
- Some packages have the option for you to purchase a dedicated URL and have a professional email address.
- Many of the sites will have instructions on how to insert details to assist search engine optimisation and will automatically produce mobile-friendly and tablet-friendly versions of your site.

The disadvantages are that you need moderate IT skills to use such sites, and the templates you choose are not uniquely yours. Your website design will be shared by others (though given the millions of websites, surfers are unlikely to encounter a design identical to yours).

At the time of writing, such online website builders include:

- Weebly (http://www.weebly.com/)
- Jimdo (http://www.jimdo.com/)
- Wix (http://www.wix.com/)
- 1&1 Mywebsite (http://www.1and1.co.uk/)

Search engine optimisation

A tree falling in a forest is probably an unremarkable event, unless it is seen by someone. Having one website amongst millions is unremarkable unless potential clients can see your website, and if it appears on page 156 of Google, your potential clients are probably not going to find it when searching for counselling. If you go to the trouble and expense of getting a website, all that is likely to be wasted unless your site is optimised for search engines.

Although the precise secrets of what helps your site rise through the ranks are closely guarded by the search engine creators, and change on a regular basis, broadly speaking there are five things that are likely to help your site get some priority over others.

- Good, relevant content. If you want to attract clients who are searching for counselling, make sure 1) that your site is exclusively about counselling and that you don't also use it to advertise your son's plumbing business, and 2) that is says something more than "I am Mrs Smith and I live at 53 Acacia Avenue and I do counselling." You might, for example, have links to other helpful material, or have articles you have written about how counselling might help particular problems.
- Relevant term density. Think about which terms potential clients might type into the box of a search engine, and make sure that those terms appear frequently in natural language on your site, especially on the first page. If clients looking for a counsellor in Boston are likely to type "counsellor in Boston" into a search engine, make sure that "counsellor" and "Boston" appear frequently on your first page. You might naturally use the terms "therapist" and "psychotherapist", but where appropriate substitute "counsellor" on your website if that is what you think potential clients will search for. And don't be afraid of using phrases such as "the Boston counsellor" or "Boston counselling".

- URL and search term matching. Most people choose the name of their business, then chose their URL, and then worry about search engine optimisation. It would be far better to be aware of search engine optimisation at the beginning and to choose your business name and URL accordingly. If potential clients are likely to search for a counsellor in Boston, having "bostoncounsellor.co.uk" as a URL would be preferable in search optimisation terms to something like "safespacecounselling.co.uk". Years ago, when I started my business (Connections Counselling Ltd), I bought what I now realise was a dreadful URL ("connections-c.co.uk") but nobody searches for my business name. I now have "kingslynncounsellor.co.uk". One of my local competitors has "counsellinginkingslynn.co.uk", and, at the time of writing, "kingslynn-counsellor.co.uk" and "thekingslynncounsellor.co.uk" are waiting to be snapped up.

- Relevant header code. The search engines like relevant terms (such as "counsellor", "counselling", "Boston") which reflect the page content inserted into the header of the page code (not the material that you see, but the HTML code behind the page that you cannot see). Website designers should be able to easily do this for you. Some of the online website builders enable you to do this easily.

- Mobile-friendly and tablet-friendly versions of your site. Because more websites are now viewed on tablets and mobile phones than on desktop machines or on laptops, some search engines (Google, for example) give preference to sites that have been specifically designed for those platforms. Therefore, it is very important to have a version of your site that favours those platforms.

CHAPTER TWENTY-EIGHT

What are outcome measures and should I use them?

An outcome measure is simply any form of measurement, typically a questionnaire, that is used to attempt to monitor progress. So in counselling, a questionnaire, on depression, for example, would be given to clients during assessment, at various points during their therapy, and then again at the end. Any improvement in scores would be used in partial support of the argument that the counselling was effective (or not).

In the last thirty years or so, there has been a change in attitude by some towards the measurement of the efficiency of certain services offered to the public. In very broad terms, it has always been "normal" for major businesses dealing with, say, the production of widgets, to measure the effectiveness of their practices. Ineffectiveness could be relatively easily measured and could be worked on in order to reduce costs. However, there now seems a more general acceptance (certainly by government) that the effectiveness of public services should be measured as well as the effectiveness of factory production and general business outcomes.

The problems are that human beings—their bodies and minds and their infinite range of interactions—are more complex and difficult to measure than machines producing widgets or shops selling groceries.

Despite possible objections and real difficulties, some would argue that there are at least five reasons for attempting to measure outcomes.

First, it could be argued that it isn't as difficult to do as is often claimed. It has been pointed out that there are some relatively clear-cut variables that could be measured (examination results and death rates, for example). In addition to this, there are relatively well-established psychometric techniques for measuring attitude, and satisfaction, and improvement in particular areas. So, for example, it is claimed that it is relatively easy to measure client satisfaction and progress. The argument goes that because it wasn't done in the past (or if it was, only within the research community) doesn't mean that it couldn't be done more widely now.

Second, it is argued that there is a moral duty to ensure that money is spent well, whether that money is public money spent by government on services, or private money spent by individual clients. In order to know whether the money is likely to be well spent, it is necessary to have some idea about how effective the service is. As a parent, you would want your child to go to the best school or the best hospital and would need relevant information to help you make that judgement. And arguably that information would be even more important if you were investing thousands of pounds in paying for private treatment in a hospital, or paying school fees at a private school. As a potential client trying to decide between around ten local counsellors, effectiveness on certain measures *might be* useful information in helping you decide which particular therapist you are going to give your money to. You don't want to waste time or money on someone who *might be* unhelpful to you.

Third, it is argued that at a national level, outcome measures and quantitative research are part of the language spoken by politicians and those determining policy and awarding funding. If counselling is to gain increasing credibility, and if private practitioners are ever going to stand a chance of being funded centrally to help contribute to the nation's mental health, then we need to start understanding and speaking that language. We may not like the language, but it may be tactically necessary to speak it to those who won't listen to us if we don't.

Fourth, there is a moral obligation to do no harm, at worst, and at best, to help clients improve. Dr Shipman, and the recent scandal at Mid-Staffordshire Hospital, sadly demonstrate what can happen when outcomes are not monitored closely. There are many in the pseudo-medical field offering treatments that scientific experts might describe as being as effective as "snake oil". The argument is that unless we monitor outcomes and changes more systematically, we as counsellors lack systematic evidence about our effectiveness.

Fifth, some outcome measures can give us information that is diagnostic and can help us improve our practice. At a very general level, repeated evidence that many clients are not improving might cause us to reflect on possible reasons. Barry Duncan and Scott Miller (https://www.psychotherapy.net/article/therapy-effectiveness/) have found that the most effective counsellors ask clients what they want and then give it to them. Some regularly used his Session Rating Scale to monitor client satisfaction, and then followed up responses in order to discover how they might improve their work with particular individuals. I use the specific information from the supervision personalisation forms developed by Wallace and Cooper http://www.roehampton.ac.uk/uploadedFiles/ Pages_Assets/PDFs_and_Word_Docs/Research_Centres/CARACAW/Therapy%20Personnalisation%20 Form%201.doc to help monitor my supervisee's experience of their supervision and learn how I might concentrate on particular areas to work more effectively with them.

Despite the arguments for trying to measure counselling outcomes and for presenting those results to the public, many counsellors profoundly object to the very idea. They argue that the possible outcomes from therapy are too complex to be reduced to a number on a psychometric scale, that the administration of measurement scales is intrusive, and that the presentation of any results gives a dishonest impression about what we do.

You must decide for yourself where you stand on the issue. My own view is that despite the difficulties and inadequacy of any measures, the profession risks being left behind and looking amateurish unless we can present some evidence for the effectiveness of what we do. However, whenever those outcomes are presented, whether that be at a national level arguing for the profession's credibility, or at the level of the individual therapist trying to get more clients, I would want there to be an honest disclosure of the following points:

- All psychometric instruments have a margin of error associated with them.
- Scores can be influenced by how the measurement tools are administered. Different conditions such as

time of day and slight variations in the instructions to the client can have an impact on results.

- Some clients would want to present more positive results than are actually the case in order not to offend the therapist or admit to themselves that the money they have spent has not delivered what they hoped for.
- Most studies using outcome measures to assess the effectiveness of counselling don't attempt to assess long-term effectiveness.
- Unless outcomes from a control group that has no counselling are also measured, it is difficult to argue that any improvement in the clients is entirely due to counselling. Their "conditions" might have improved with the passing of time anyway, without counselling.
- Any score is always going to be an extremely partial representation of the changes that may have taken place in the client. Scores are always an incomplete picture.
- There should be a degree of tentativeness about the presentation of results.

If you decide to use outcome measures to monitor your progress, you should familiarise yourself with the following information:

- Whether or not the measure is free to use. Not all tests are free for general use, though many are. Some are free to use provided that the copyright conditions are strictly adhered to. You should not use a test dishonestly if its usage requires payment of a licence fee to the developers.
- What the specific instructions are for administering the questionnaire. If these instructions are not followed, any results are invalid. So, for example, one commonly used questionnaire (PHQ-9, see below)

asks clients to rate how they have felt during the previous fortnight, and yet I have come across one person who uses the form for asking the clients how they have felt during the previous week. A difference of seven days can make a considerable difference to the scores. You also need to be consistent in your administration. Use the forms either at the beginning or end of the session with each client, but don't vary the occasion, as this will also have an impact on the outcomes.

- Carefully read any information provided by the developers to help you interpret what the scores may mean.

What measures could I use?

There are a range of measures available, with new ones being developed all the time. The list below is meant to be illustrative of a few rather than a definitive list.

PHQ-9

The Patient Health Questionnaire is a nine-item questionnaire for measuring depression. Clients respond to statements by saying how frequently they have felt what the statement describes during the previous fortnight. The score could then be used to assess the level of depression (none, mild, moderate, moderately severe, severe). It is used extensively within the NHS, and clients may have already come across it without realising as it is frequently used by GPs when patients present themselves as feeling depressed. (http:// patient.info/doctor/patient-health-questionnaire-phq-9).

GAD-7

The General Anxiety Disorder Assessment is a seven-item questionnaire for measuring anxiety. Clients respond to statements by saying how frequently they have felt what the statement describes during the previous fortnight. The score could then be used to assess the level of anxiety—none, mild, moderate, severe. (http://patient.info/doctor/generalised-anxiety-disorder-assessment-gad-700).

CORE-10

This is the ten-item shortened version of the CORE OM, which is a thirty-four-item generic measure of psychological distress. Clients respond to statements by saying how frequently they have felt what the statement describes during the previous week. The ten-item version covers anxiety, depression, trauma, physical problems, relationship functioning, and risk to self. (http://www.coreims.co.uk/About_Measurement_CORE_Tools.html).

Satisfaction with life scale

Clients are asked how strongly they agree or disagree with five statements about life. (http://internal.psychology.illinois.edu/~ediener/SWLS.html).

WEMWBS

The Warwick-Edinburgh Mental Well-Being Scale is a fourteen-item scale used in NHS Scotland. Clients respond to statements by saying how frequently they have felt what the statement describes during the previous fortnight. (http://www.healthscotland.com/scotlands-health/population/Measuring-positive-mental-health.aspx).

QIDS-SR16

The Beck Depression Inventory, while very popular, is not free to use. The Quick Inventory of Depressive Symptomatology is a free alternative that has the potential to yield useful diagnostic information as well as a score. Clients are asked to assess the frequency/intensity of their symptoms in response to sixteen questions. (http://www.ids-qids.org/).

NovoPsych

For counsellors who have access to a tablet computer, there are several apps on the market that enable to therapist to present the client with a particular outcome measure on screen to enable the client to just press the relevant box. Most apps will then present the user with a score. At the time of writing, one of the most professionally useful apps in this area is the NovoPsych Psychology iPad App (http://www.novopsych.com/) for Administering Psychometric Tests and Questionnaires. It has several useful features:

- Its bank of outcome measures include: Depression Anxiety Stress Scales (both the DASS-42 and DASS-21), Generalised Anxiety Disorder 7-item (GAD-7), Patient Health Questionnaire—Depression (PHQ-9), Kessler Psychological Distress Scale (K10), Panic Disorder Severity Scale (PDSS), Social Interaction Anxiety Scale (SIAS), Edinburgh Postnatal Depression Scale (EPDS), Autism Spectrum

Screening Questionnaire (ASSQ), Scale of Positive and Negative Experience (SPANE), Rosenberg Self-Esteem Scale (RSES), Social Avoidance and Distress Scale (SADS), Vancouver Obsessional Compulsive Inventory (VOCI).

- The bank currently has over forty free-to-use measures, and these are being added to all the time.
- There is easy access to the industry standard tests as well as relevant psychometric information.
- The measures are easy to administer. There is no need to worry about maintaining a supply of test papers, instruction sheets, and pens. You simply select the measure and then pass the tablet to the client.
- Scores are instantly available in app or can be emailed to the therapist. For many of the most popular tests, several results can be stored and presented in the app in a graphical format so that the client and the therapist can easily monitor progress.
- The technology is built using above industry standard encryption technology.

CHAPTER TWENTY-NINE

What is a professional will and do I need one?

A professional will is simply a plan of what you want to happen in the event of you being suddenly incapacitated in any way and unable to carry on (permanently or temporarily) running your therapy business.

A counsellor experienced a major medical event that resulted in her being rushed to hospital and unable to work for some time—these things happen. Her diary had fifteen therapy appointments lined up for the coming week, and she had around twenty "active" clients on her books (some of whom were seeing her fortnightly or intermittently).

The medical emergency could have resulted in administrative and professional chaos. Her partner was in no emotional state to shoulder the load. Clients could have continually turned up at the house only to be turned away at best, or left standing in puzzlement at worst. New requests for appointments would have kept coming in. And clients would have been left in a therapeutic limbo, which would have been detrimental for many of them, and certainly wouldn't have provided them with a high standard of care.

Fortunately, this therapist had thought through what she might do in such eventualities and had had discussions with two reliable colleagues. And fortunately, although she had not written things down, she was sufficiently conscious to ask her partner to activate the plan.

She was able to give one colleague her passwords, which enabled the colleague to access her computer and retrieve the encrypted client details for all the future appointments in her diary. This colleague also changed the message on the answerphone to say that the therapist would not be offering any future appointments until further notice and giving details of how potential clients could access details of other possible therapists via a web address. The two colleagues then shared responsibility for immediately contacting the booked clients (or the EAPs, companies, or rehabilitation agencies concerned) via telephone to try to speak to the person concerned, rather than leave a message. The intended message was: apologies for the inconvenience; all future appointments would be cancelled with immediate effect; the counsellor was likely to be indisposed for at least one month; information on how alternative registered local counsellors (if required) could be accessed; giving the Samaritans phone number; offering clients the option of phoning back after a calendar month to see whether the therapist would be back at work in case they wanted to wait.

These arrangements did go some way to preventing chaos and demonstrating some care for the clients. However, the arrangements were *not* perfect, and perhaps they never can be. But as a result of what happened, the therapist is in the process of doing the following:

- Reviewing the previous arrangements with her two colleagues and checking their continued willingness to act in future.
- Writing down precisely what she wants to happen and who she wishes to do what, and giving those wishes to her partner and willing colleagues.
- Meeting with all of the above and ensuring that they have written instructions, including written details of how to access her confidential, encrypted client details.

All of the above will help deal with the immediate effect of a disaster temporarily disrupting your business, but what about if you died suddenly through illness or accident? What if your business needed to be closed down? The above instructions would help deal with the clients, but what about the other aspects of your business?

One of the things this therapist is in the process of doing is asking someone to act as a kind of business executor; someone to help her partner to close down the business. The tasks are likely to include:

- liaising with any accountant;
- paying any outstanding bills;
- stopping monthly outgoings and any rental agreements on the business account;
- liaising to close down the business bank account and cancel business insurance;
- withdrawing any online presence.

Once she has chosen whom to ask, she will again make a written list of the things she would hope would be done if the chosen person were able and willing to do that.

Whoever carries out the wishes of the counsellor— whether it be one or more person—they do deserve to be paid. Any agreement needs to take into account both the level and process of remuneration, and that needs to be written down too.

Of course, the above agreements do not have the legal force of a formal last will and testament, usually drawn up by a solicitor. The latter is usually concerned with distribution of personal assets. The above agreements are informal agreements, dependent on the good will of friends and colleagues, attempting to pragmatically prevent problems and help mitigate the inevitable effects of a disaster of some kind.

If you were not in private practice and were working for an organisation, there would probably be clear procedures to follow in the event of your sudden unavailability, and there would certainly be other colleagues to do all the necessary actions. However, that support network is not there if you work by yourself. It is almost certainly part of your duty of care to think about what would happen if you suddenly became unavailable and to enlist the support of trusted others in order to have concrete plans in place.

CHAPTER THIRTY

How can I increase access to my services?*

I f there had been lots of private practitioners around in the early twentieth century when cars started to become popular, I suspect that at least one coun-sellor would have had a few suspicions. Humour me and imagine the thinking.

"I feel uneasy about cars. We should be cautious about encouraging clients to come to us using them. They are dirty and dangerous. Counsellors shouldn't have anything to do with things which are so morally repugnant. They can kill people. They could be used to bring all sorts of strange people to our consulting rooms, especially at times when we don't want them. Young people and adulterers could have sex in them. They will encourage the breakdown of family life and decent values. I'm certainly not going to learn to drive one. My penny-farthing will do just fine, thank you!"

---

*A version of this answer initially appeared in Rye, J. (2014). Breaking down barriers. *Private Practice*, Summer: 29–30. Used with BACP's kind permission.

Fast-forward a few years to the growth in telephone usage. "I'm not sure that we should be encouraging clients to use the telephone to book appointments. After all, they could be playing games with us and pretending to be someone different. They might call us up at any time and that might be inconvenient for us and breaking all sorts of boundaries. I think it is important to be able to see their face and body language when they book an appointment—for me, it's part of the assessment. Can you imagine it? If we started taking appointments over the phone, someone will soon start saying that we could actually do counselling using the device. Whatever next? Thank goodness for the postage stamp and the front door!"

Of course, I am fully aware that cars and telephones can be dangerous and used for all sorts of evil purposes. I also know that I use a car and a telephone on a daily basis, that I am glad of the benefits that they bring to me, and that as a counsellor, life would be much more difficult without them. Imagine if all appointments had to be made via snailmail, and if all clients had to walk to me or arrive in a horse-drawn carriage.

One of the biggest surprises for me when I started out in private practice was how technology brought me clients I had never dreamed I would be able to work with. Before I illustrate that statement, I need to make two points.

First, I am not unaware that any technology can have a downside. It can greatly facilitate verbal and visual communication, and that can be enriching (as a grandparent, I can "FaceTime" my young grandchildren before they go to bed, even though we are some distance apart), or it can be used in ways that society would generally (and publicly, at least) disapprove of (facilitating titillating illicit sexual liaisons underneath the noses of existing partners). I am very aware that telephone or internet counselling are not the same as face-to-face counselling. And, of course, I am aware of the need to take reasonable steps to ascertain the true identity of clients who may not be physically present, and aware of the need to get relevant permissions so that I would be able to exercise an appropriate level of care if safeguarding issues ever arose. I am aware that a client who is present on a video screen is not the same as a client who is present in the room. I am aware that there are difficulties over confidentiality and security. I am aware that there might be difficulties and restrictions over insurance. (See, for example, *Ethical Framework for the Use of Social Media by Mental Health Professionals*, http://onlinetherapyinstitute.com/ethical-framework-for-the-use-of-social-media-by-mental-health-professionals/.) However, these are issues that need to be recognised and solved. "Different" is not necessarily "bad"—just "different".

Second, when I started out in private practice, I came from a working life where I had spent a long time using technology to break down access barriers, and to have significant "pastoral" and academic interactions with adults. I regularly worked with individuals or small groups using the telephone, or the relatively new means of email, chat rooms, electronic forums, and video conferencing. One of the institutions where I worked was actively developing one of the first degree programmes to be delivered entirely online (both academic material, student–tutor interaction, and student–student interaction). At the time, it seemed natural for me to use new technology to interact with adults, and it seemed odd that more counsellors weren't doing this.

So I started my private practice. I knew that most of my work would be face to face, but I also made it known that I would be willing to do email, telephone, internet chat, and video-call work. Below are just a few fictitious examples, based on real experiences, of working with technology.

Sally's story

Sally was a very intelligent but nervous lady who lived in a town about sixty miles from my home. She wanted to work on her anxiety, on her relationship with her partner, and on a big decision she had to make. She originally contacted me via email, and I sent six coun- selling emails in response to her emails. There was a pause for about a month, and then I received an email from her saying that she wanted to book a telephone counselling session. This was arranged, and over the course of the next month, we had three telephone ses- sions. After that, her "final" two sessions were face to face—partly because her confidence in herself, in me, and in the process had grown sufficiently for her to make the journey and be physically present, and partly, I suspect, because she was just curious to see who it was to whom she had been revealing her inner turmoil.

Although comparatively brief, it was a satisfying piece of work. Sally had shown significant growth in confidence, was beginning to deal with some of the issues in her relationship with her partner, and had made the big decision: to leave this country and to move to the Netherlands. She has said that she could never have braved a face-to-face encounter to begin with, and even if she had done, she would never have opened up. The flexible use of different technology enabled her to put a toe into the counselling experi- ence water and grow as a result.

About two years later, I received a phone call from the Netherlands. Sally had settled and was glad she had made the decision to move. However, her relationship with her partner had now ended and she wanted to return to counselling. Accessing a counsellor she trusted and who knew part of her story seemed the natural thing to do. The fact that I was in a different country and that we were working via Skype seemed almost irrelevant.

Maryanne and Tom's story

Maryanne and Tom lived in a large city "up North". They had been together for seven years and had a four-year-old son. Tom was a much travelled engineer and had met Maryanne on a trip to Malta. Several flights later, they were married, parents, and living in the UK. However, when Tom initially contacted me, their relationship had deteriorated and they were looking to see if they could "save their marriage". Tom told me that he was about to depart to the Middle East for a six-month work period and that Maryanne had taken their son back to "Mum" in Malta. My initial thoughts were that couple counselling over the phone would be "challenging", and that it couldn't be attempted until they were both together. However, Tom questioned that. He was used to conference calls. Why couldn't we set up a three-way conference call between the Malta, UK, and Saudi Arabia?

Although getting the timings right was a nightmare, in the end we did have five conference calls over a two-month period. Tom and Maryanne were not able to solve their problems, but in our sessions there were times when they were able to talk openly without fighting and resolve some issues. The whole experience reminded me that "challenging" doesn't mean "impossible", and again, that "different" is just "different".

Increasing access

Several clients in the UK have only come to counselling because of a technology. These kind of clients may be familiar to many of you. Sometimes they are people who have agoraphobia, possibly bullied at school, who never (or very rarely) go out, not even to the doctors. Or perhaps they are people who lost their job years ago and consequently have lost all confidence and cannot face people. Some of them do everything online. They certainly wouldn't want to physically attend a counselling session, yet they want help and are willing to try working on the phone or via Skype or via PlusGuidance.

Other UK clients are often people who have a different kind of limitation affecting their access to therapy. There are the mums who couldn't travel to counselling because of time restrictions and childcare, but who could fit in telephone sessions on rare occasions when they are not on "parent duty". Occasionally, I work with clients who live in remote communities and who are unwilling or unable to travel to therapy. The group that surprised me the most were those who chose to use technology in order to feel safe away from their community. If you are a female vicar using male prostitutes behind your husband's back, or two GPs in the same practice having an affair, you may know several of the local counsellors and their supervisors. Although your fears about a potential confidentiality breech are hopefully unfounded, you feel safer accessing help outside the community where you live and work.

The largest group of clients I have worked with using technology are members of the growing British community living and working abroad. Such people may not have sufficient local language skill (if any) to feel comfortable about engaging in therapeutic dialogue. The sound of home is literally more attractive and comforting. And of course, in certain places, appropriate professional therapy may not be available.

The fictitious list below illustrates typical clients from this last group:

- an anxious executive being bullied in an international company in Switzerland;
- a depressed academic teaching in a South Korean university;
- a stressed charity worker in Romania;
- a couple working as aid workers in Africa, trying to hold their marriage together;
- a grieving widower in Italy whose wife had died soon after they had sold up in the UK and moved abroad;
- an angry pensioner in Spain whose husband had run off with the lawyer dealing with the purchase of their retirement property;
- a depressed and anxious businesswoman in Greece who was facing bankruptcy;
- a factory manager from Thailand who wanted to work with his partner to improve their relationship.

All of the above were UK nationals and were able to access therapy because of a willingness to work using technology.

Not only can technology link counsellors and clients, but it can also link counsellors and their supervisors. If they are willing to work with technology, counsellors can now access supervision beyond the confines of their local community. So, for example, I now have supervisees who originally came to me when they lived near me, but who now continue to work with me even though they have moved to different parts of the country. My own supervisor lives hundreds of miles away from me, but I chose him because his particular experience and expertise was a better match for what I was looking for than those I could have accessed locally.

I don't know what private practice will look like in fifty years' time. Our core models may have been modified in the light of research. However, with regard to using technology to interact with clients, I feel reasonably confident that what today seems odd to some people will be much more normal and routine, and that those counselling business owners with a tendency to think outside the box will have new boxes to challenge them.

CHAPTER THIRTY-ONE

What is the difference between a sole trader and a limited company?

While most counsellors are happy to function as sole traders, a few will decide to form their own limited companies. There are advantages and disadvantages to both business structures, and to some extent, particular advantages may be dependent on any particular tax regime at the time. For example, when one chancellor announced in a budget that he was abandoning any tax on the first £10,000 of a limited company's profit, many hundreds of thousands of sole traders, many of whom ran very small businesses and would not normally have thought of operating as a limited company, were advised by their accountants to become company directors in a successful move to wipe out all, or most of, their tax bill. Sadly, other chancellors have since reversed that decision.

I have found it helpful to think of the difference between the two structures under four headings.

Liability

If you are a sole trader, you are liable for any claims against the company and for any debts of the company. You are the company. So, if your company owes £10,000, but you only have £5,000 in the company bank account, you would be liable to pay the remaining £5,000 out of your own money. It is easy to see how some sole traders, particularly those having to spend significant money on materials in order to trade (builders, for example) could become personally bankrupt if their business debts grew too large.

If you trade as a limited company, the company itself exists as a legal entity in its own right, and any claims against it are limited to the resources of the company. You are not the company, but an officer of the company. If your company owes £10,000, but it only has £5,000 in the company bank account, it could only pay half of its debt (though its resources could be sold to contribute to the rest). However, you would not be liable to make up any difference from your personal financial resources. Trading as a limited company is a protection against personal bankruptcy—a reason why a few counsellors elect to trade in this way, rather than as sole traders.

Flexibility

If you are a sole trader, you pay yourself a wage by taking drawings out of the company. If you trade as a limited company, the company can employ you (because it exists in its own right) and pay you a wage. However, if you set the company up, you will own shares in the company and you could elect to pay yourself a dividend for the shares that you own. You could pay yourself with a combination of a wage and dividends.

Limited companies' directors have the potential to pay less tax, as they can pay themselves small salaries and high dividends which are free from National Insurance. However, sole traders pay themselves a salary that is liable for NICs as well as income tax.

Registration and paperwork

If you are a sole trader, you simply have to register with HMRC and keep a good set of accounts.

If you form a limited company, there is a lot more paperwork involved. You have to complete the company registration forms and submit them to Companies House. You have to name the director(s) of the company, and you must have a company secretary (someone officially responsible for the paperwork). In small companies (most therapy businesses), directors can also be company secretaries. Once registered, your company name is protected; no other business can use it.

There are more obligations on limited company directors than on sole traders. They have to hold at least one formal meeting a year (even if there is only one director), and submit minutes and their accounts to Companies House. These accounts are public, and for a small fee, anyone can access them.

Despite the paperwork involved in setting up and maintaining a limited company, some people feel that the advantages are worth the effort. There are plenty of people around to help with the paperwork. If you do not wish to create and register the company yourself, your accountant may do it for you, or there are plenty of firms on the internet offering to complete the necessary paperwork and send the documents to you (sometimes complete with a business bank account) in a few days. And most accountants would be willing to complete and submit the annual accounts and minutes from the director's meeting.

Expense

On the face of it, there is initially more expense involved in trading as a limited company than as a sole trader. You have to pay limited company set-up fees and ongoing registration costs. Your accountant will charge you marginally more for preparing accounts for a limited company than for a sole trader, your personal liability insurance firm may charge you more for a limited company (some won't), and if you have no other income, you *may* end up paying more in company corporation tax than you would have done in income tax as a sole trader (it depends on your individual financial circumstances).

Despite the initial higher expense, some business owners feel the slightly higher cost of a limited company is worth it for the limitation of liabilities, the greater flexibility of remuneration, and the possible added prestige of owning one. It is also worth remembering that National Insurance obligations on limited companies can be lower than on sole traders, and that once turnover reaches a certain point (somewhere between £15,000 and £20,000), it could become less expensive to trade as a limited company.

Seek advice

Clearly, the decision whether to trade as a sole trader or a limited company isn't simple. There are plenty of websites explaining the difference between the two. A chat with your accountant will take on board your personal financial circumstance and help you work out what is best for you. The good news is that the decision isn't set in concrete and you can change between the two if necessary. It is not uncommon for people to start out as sole traders and then move to forming limited companies.

Although sole trader and limited companies are the most likely structures for your business, there are others available. (See: https://www.gov.uk/business-legal-structures.)